I'M DREAMING OF

A BLACK CHRISTMAS

❄

ALSO BY LEWIS BLACK

Me of Little Faith

Nothing's Sacred

Riverhead Books

New York

I'M DREAMING OF
A BLACK CHRISTMAS

✳

LEWIS BLACK

RIVERHEAD BOOKS
Published by the Penguin Group
Penguin Group (USA) Inc.
375 Hudson Street, New York, New York 10014, USA
Penguin Group (Canada), 90 Eglinton Avenue East, Suite 700, Toronto, Ontario M4P 2Y3, Canada
(a division of Pearson Penguin Canada Inc.)
Penguin Books Ltd., 80 Strand, London WC2R 0RL, England
Penguin Group Ireland, 25 St. Stephen's Green, Dublin 2, Ireland (a division of Penguin Books Ltd.)
Penguin Group (Australia), 250 Camberwell Road, Camberwell, Victoria 3124, Australia
(a division of Pearson Australia Group Pty. Ltd.)
Penguin Books India Pvt. Ltd., 11 Community Centre, Panchsheel Park, New Delhi—110 017, India
Penguin Group (NZ), 67 Apollo Drive, Rosedale, Auckland 0632, New Zealand
(a division of Pearson New Zealand Ltd.)
Penguin Books (South Africa) (Pty.) Ltd., 24 Sturdee Avenue, Rosebank, Johannesburg 2196,
South Africa

Penguin Books Ltd., Registered Offices: 80 Strand, London WC2R 0RL, England

The publisher does not have any control over and does not assume any responsibility for author or
third-party websites or their content.

First Riverhead hardcover edition: November 2010
First Riverhead trade paperback edition: November 2011
Riverhead trade paperback ISBN: 978-1-59448-542-8

The Library of Congress has catalogued the Riverhead hardcover edition as follows:

Black, Lewis, date.
I'm dreaming of a black Christmas / Lewis Black.
p. cm.
ISBN 978-1-59448-775-0
1. Christmas—Humor. 2. American wit and humor. I. Title.
PN 6231.C36B57   2010   2010025846
814'.6—dc22

PRINTED IN THE UNITED STATES OF AMERICA

10 9 8 7 6 5 4 3 2

To my mentors:

George Carlin, Kurt Vonnegut, Professor William Geer,

and my uncle, Julius Kaplan

CONTENTS

I'M DREAMING OF
A BLACK CHRISTMAS

❄

INTRODUCTION

The Uplifting and Heartfelt Story of How This Book Came to Be

No, your eyes are not deceiving you. This is a book about Christmas (or the "holiday season," if you're deranged enough that you have to call it that), written by your old friend, the essence of the Christmas Spirit, Mr. Mirth himself, me.

How did this come to pass? How did this glorious miracle occur? What star in the East was seen by yours truly that inspired him to write this book?

Well, now, *there's* a story.

Every memorable Christmas story has its beginnings in the yearnings of the heart. Not mine, of course. But somebody else's. I have naps to take, after all. In truth, Dear Reader, it wasn't my idea to subject you to my deepest, most personal feelings about this time of year. I know better than that.

A while ago I was having lunch with my editor, who over the bread basket turned to me, his youthful eyes filled with hope, and asked, "Any thoughts on a new book?"

Right. Like I had been devoting all of my spare time to coming up with a concept for a book that would keep me chained to my desk for the next year, pining for a real life that was just outside my window.

"Not a one," I replied happily. "Besides, I thought I'd brought book publishing to its knees with my last one. Ever since that book came out, your industry has been in a tailspin."

"Really?" he asked. "I thought that was the recession and the shifting technological landscape." (Yes, he really does talk like that.) "Did you cause those, too? By the way, can I have your breadstick?"

"No. I want it. Besides, nobody reads anymore. People have no time for that kind of stuff. What's important now is a constant flow of vital information that one can access instantaneously. You know, like who has a new blog"— Christ, I hate that word—"or a new sex tape for sale."

"Are you sure you want that breadstick?"

"For crying out loud, no one wants a whole book of thoughts or some fictional flight of fantasy," I continue as I crunch on a breadstick I don't want. "People want things in real time. They want to know where to eat, to shop, to drink. They want it to be close. They want to know how to fucking get there. And if the phone would tell them who to fuck, they'd go and fuck them, and I mean that on all levels of the word. *And they want to know right now,* not by chapter 7. It could be too late by then. For God's sake, there are Twitter books. How can that even be? But it is. We are getting to the point where authors won't even have to write, THEY'LL INSTALL A CHIP IN THEIR HEADS AND THEN YOU CAN GO TO WHOEVER GETS THE TECHNOLOGY FIRST AND THEN YOU CAN JUST LISTEN TO THE BOOK AS THE AUTHOR THINKS IT! TALK TO ME AGAIN ABOUT A BOOK WHEN YOU HAVE A CHIP INSTALLED IN *THIS*!"

I punctuated my point by pounding my head, which actually quieted the voices in my head for a minute or two.

"Are you finished?" my editor asked quietly.

"You're the one who's finished."

"Did you hurt yourself?" he pressed on. "Do I need to call somebody?"

"What are you, a Boy Scout? No, I don't need anybody called."

"You insist on pounding your head like that, you're going to do damage. More damage than you've already done, I mean," he added.

"Never mind. It's like a pinball machine up there. I'm just whacking it to get it out of the tilt mode."

"I have an idea," he said.

"An idea? Are you kidding me? Seriously. Ideas are

the next thing to go. We are moving rapidly into a world of ideacons. They're like those stupid emoticons, only they pretend to express an idea. Just like you don't have to feel the emotion, pretty soon you won't have to be bothered by thinking, either."

"That's good. Save it for the page."

"The page? Are you talking about paper? You're killing me here. It's all going to be on a screen."

"It's still a book."

"What book?"

"The one you should write about Christmas."

"Are you out of your fucking mind? A Christmas book based on all the memories I don't have of it, because, lest you forget, I am a Jew."

"Lewis, Dickens was a Jew."

"No, he wasn't."

"He wanted to be."

"Not at Christmastime, he didn't."

"That's your book."

"That's not a book. It's barely a sentence." The voices in my head were starting to clear their throats again.

"Glenn Beck wrote a Christmas book."

"You've got to be kidding me. Called what? *Santa's a Tubby Socialist*, where Glenn analyzes why a fat man—dressed in red, no less—distributes gifts to every single child to teach them the heinous act of sharing? I've got news for you: Santa doesn't bring anything for the Jewish kids, because they already worship a Socialist God of their own. I'm sure Glenn's even got a chapter about how President Obama believes in Santa more than the country he may or may not have been born in."

"Not even close, Lewis. But if Glenn Beck can write a book for Christmas, so can you."

"And as every mom used to say, 'If Glenn jumped off a roof, would you?' "

"Well, if I could get his publishing rights, I would. But I know you can write a better book about Christmas, Lewis."

"You son of a bitch, taunting me with Glenn Beck. If I can't write a better book than he does, I should jump off the roof. What makes you think I should write a book about Christmas?"

"You've been Santa twice. They asked you to play Scrooge in a huge production of *A Christmas Carol*."

Yes, you read that correctly: me as Scrooge. My career, Dear Reader, has been a strange one, with twists and turns as weird as anything cooked up by Stephen King or the writers of *The Hills*. But playing Scrooge, that was truly an odd one. As far as I know, no one I have known in my forty years in the professional theater ever even considered the possibility of my playing Dickens's most famous Christmas-hater. (Or if somebody had thought of the idea, he'd mentioned it to someone else and the other person had died laughing.)

If the casting wasn't strange enough, the play's producers were offering me a small fortune to play the role, in huge theaters around the country. (The reason I mention that they were willing to pay me a bunch of money that felt to me like the kind of money you get in pro sports is that at the time the economy was tanking—badly. *A Christmas Carol* starring Lewis Black as Scrooge—it sounds like the producers were Bialy-stock and Bloom from *The Producers*. Theoretically it makes a bit of sense. I mean, who better to play Scrooge than a bitter, angry Jew?)

As ludicrous as the whole idea was, it didn't stop me from picking up the script and looking at it. (And who knew what might follow if it worked? Lewis Black as King Lear? Lewis Black as Macbeth? Lewis Black as Mama Rose in *Gypsy*?) As I read, I was shocked to find out how big Scrooge's part is. Somehow I remembered it as just a bunch of "Humbugs" with an occasional "Bah" thrown in to spice things up. Nope, Ebenezer yacks a lot. More than is really necessary, to be honest. He goes on and on and *on and* ON, in order to show everybody what a prick he is. I might have had a stroke memorizing all that shit.

Fortunately for my few remaining brain cells, the show never happened. The producers couldn't find a cast that could help me sell enough tickets for the thing to make financial sense.

Which is why I'm sitting at lunch yelling at my editor about Glenn Beck. "You know, I didn't end up playing Scrooge."

"And that's my fault? Come on, Lewis. This is better than being Scrooge. You can write about him. You can talk about how you would have been the definitive Scrooge. How you would have been remembered for your work, like that actor Booth was."

"Because he killed Lincoln."

"No, the other one. Shirley, I think her name was."

"I wouldn't have been the definitive Scrooge."

"Then tell them why you would have been a lousy Scrooge. Tell them whatever you want. It's your book."

"I don't want to write another book. I don't have to write another book. Writing is hell. It's brutal. It's hours of sitting by myself in front of a piece-of-shit computer, spewing out my guts and then dealing with you and your whiny notes. '*You need a better joke here. I don't understand this paragraph. This doesn't make sense.*'"

"I don't give whiny notes."

"All notes are whiny."

"Lewis. Listen to me. If you write another book, the public might begin to believe you are a writer."

Son of a bitch! Now he got me. I've always wanted to be known as a writer. It's why I went to graduate school, for crying out loud.

And then I realized: This guy's not my editor. He's a crack dealer for my self-esteem.

"I don't know if I can do it."

"Of course you can. You're a writer."

"Stop it. It's like you're rubbing the inner thigh of my brain."

"Think about it. Take long walks. Let your mind run free. We'll have another lunch soon to talk about it some more."

Another free lunch. God, I love free lunches.

"Okay."

So now he's hooked me. How does he know I'll write a good book about the holidays when I didn't even think I could write another book? And why would I want to go through the tortures of the damned to finish it?

I didn't take long walks, but I thought about it. And after a while I told him that I couldn't write the kind of Christmas book that everyone else writes, and that even if I could, I wouldn't want to. Then I told him what I thought I might be able to write about.

And you know what that idiot said?

He said it's a book.

I hope he's right, because here it is.

A WARNING TO THE READER
FROM THE AUTHOR

Before you proceed, I want you to know that for those of you who have a deep attachment to the season that runs from Thanksgiving to Christmas, or an emotional connection to stores that sell Christmas stuff all year round, don't read this book. These pages aren't where you want to be. I am telling you as a friend. Books that will make you shit fruitcakes and gingerbread men and eggnog and holly are everywhere. They surround you like Christmas music in the elevator. This book has nothing to do with you, or with those of you for whom this holiday is one of the cornerstones you rest your life on. You'll just make harrumphy noises when you read it. You won't laugh. And you'll end up hating me. I don't need that.

This book is really for the rest of us.

A COUPLE MORE PROVISOS

This book contains, like the celebration of Christmas, only 2 percent religion. Think of it as the yuletide equivalent of low-fat milk.

This book also contains what some people call profanity. I think they're full of shit.

'TIS THE SEASON

❄

And so it begins anew each year, sometimes as early as August, or as late as just before Thanksgiving. Off in the distance we hear the faint sound of bells, a muffled drumbeat, and a barely audible choir humming in harmony. What are those sounds? They're the first sounds of Christmas, the carols that we can't wait to hear, and they will be played into oblivion until our eardrums rebel in rage, screaming for silence.

And is that an elf I see? By George, it is! But, for crying out loud, it's Labor Day.

Whenever it starts, though, the Christmas season takes on a momentum all its own, like the running of the bulls. It stampedes through every street in every town, into every shop, every home, and every life, careening through our every waking moment. If we could harness its power, we would never again have to argue about fossil fuels or debate energy policy or worry about our carbon assprint.)

As this is happening, we Jews stand back and watch in awe. We are like the spectators who stand outside the fence and watch those idiots who have chosen to run with the bulls. And like many of you Christians at Christmastime, the runners are drunk and not thinking clearly. You and they are both trying to find the courage to overcome the fear of being gored, either by a bull or by an emotional verbal hatchet thrown at you by a loved one.

Why would you subject yourself to this kind of madness? Maybe that's why we Jews are called the chosen people. Because we don't have to celebrate Christmas, we only have to compete with it. And we don't really even do that, as Chanukah is proof that we just gave up.

What's extraordinary about this time of year to me is that not only has this year's Christmas arrived, it's as if every other Christmas that has ever happened before came along, too—the memory of every single one. And it's not even just your own Christmas memories; it's everybody's. Christmas during the Korean Conflict. The Christmas truce of World War I. Christmas in Bucharest. Christmas during the Middle Ages. Christmas at the White House. The list is endless.

And if that weren't enough, there are even fictional memories. *White Christmas*, the movie and the song. *How the Grinch Stole Christmas.* (As I recall, that was some kind of hedge-fund Ponzi scheme.) *A Very Brady Christmas.* Or Norman Rockwell's compendium of Christmastime paintings and magazine covers that made every American look as if they were made of cream cheese.

So many Christmas memories to contend with, so little time and emotional wherewithal to deal with them, it's an overload. Christmas isn't a holiday, it's an emotional tsunami that hits you with a wave of tinsel that engulfs you until you have drowned in a sea of good cheer.

Every year, all of that unimaginable pressure of finding just the right gift, of seeing everybody in the family, of putting up the decorations, writing the Christmas cards, selecting the perfect tree and decorating it just so, the endless lists of lists of lists—it's unbelievable. And it's extraordinary to watch. Whenever I have celebrated the holiday in the homes of others, there is a feeling that hangs over the event, that this Christmas has to be the best one ever, the most ideal, the one like that Christmas when you were young and the world seemed so sweet and you were so innocent. To get back to that time that once was but really never was what you thought it was, because it wasn't like that. It was just another Christmas and all that that entails.

As I'm a Jew, one would think I could easily escape this maelstrom, but I never do. No one can. No one is immune from the all-consuming madness. There is something that stirs deep within me as Christmas approaches. As the days tick by, an aural wall of "carols" is erected around me; the advertising on radio, television, and the Web becomes one long primal scream of sales beyond human comprehension, the holiday films flicker deep into my psyche, and the Christmas cards roll in, and with them the long laborious notes that share the joys and triumphs of the many brilliant offspring of my friends and acquaintances. This is followed by a litany of diseases wrestled with over the past year, the pets that have passed on, the minute descriptions of wondrous vacations, the occasional work promotion, all of which ends with the usual conclusion that we really need to see each other more often, like before we drop dead or something.

The most extraordinary card I ever received was a picture of a family and I had absolutely no idea of who they were. Not a one. The signature gave no clue, as it was illegible. I went through the Rolodex in my skull and came up with nothing. Who the fuck are these people in this photo and why are they so happy to see me? What kind of an asshole am I that I can no longer remember close friends? No, please, dear God, don't let it be early-onset Alzheimer's. I put the picture up on my bathroom mirror and studied it every day. Maybe his hair changed color, or maybe I know the woman from some long past drug-induced bacchanal. People just don't send these cards out willy-nilly. Maybe *that's* who they are.

Willy and Nilly. Every day I was reminded that I had a very special friend, and that I had consigned whoever it was to some dustbin in my brain. I was taunted and tortured by the photo. Until, that is, one day, when I'm in my agent's office in Los Angeles and the very old friend walks into the office I'm sitting in. Jesus, he wasn't an old friend at all. He was an agent. An agent I had met exactly once before. And his name had both a "wein" and a "stein" in it, and that was the most disturbing part of the whole episode. I received a Christmas card marking the birth of the Christ from a fellow Jew. Whom I barely knew. That's when I learned a valuable lesson: *Never* underestimate the power of a Christmas card.

As I have grown older, in the midst of all these stimuli, I find myself getting sadder and sadder. Yet the sadness is oddly comforting, as the memories flow in of my brother and the many friends whom I spent these holiday times with but who are no longer with us. For in the midst of the sense of loss and the tears, these times remembered bring a sense of joy. For some inexplicable reason these memories are conjured up by the Christmas season, though they have nothing at all to do with the holiday. Go figure.

At this time of year I find myself falling into a condition that I like to call *Infectious romanticus* or *Sentimentalicous irrationalico*. I find Christians suffer from the same condition during this time of year. The difference is, I have no remote connection to Christmas, other than as a spectator.

I shall repeat. I am A JEW. I may have been brought into Christian households to celebrate the festivities, but I am not a part of them. Christians don't seem to get why we Jews don't just embrace Christmas. Well, it's because WE DON'T BUY THE STORY! We don't believe a special infant was born and that he was the Son of God, and that story is the reason all of you Christians aren't Jews. So we are put off a little by all of the hoopla, which is perfectly understandable when you people do it, but it still makes us cringe a little.

Which makes it all the more strange that during this season I am drowning in sentimentality just like any Christian. I will choke up while watching a commercial where a father and son argue over a cell-phone plan. Tears come as a mother talks to the camera about the extraordinary power of a cleansing detergent. Coke celebrates the Christmas season with images of traditional Christmases, or Santa placing gifts under a tree, and I am incapable of getting out of my chair for a good five minutes. Someone as emotionally detached from the world as I usually am finds himself awash in emotions generally found only in movies with Jimmy Stewart in them. I am drenched in a romantic sense of life that I don't even believe in. As happy as I am with my life— okay, happy might be a bit of a stretch, but I do like my life (colonoscopies not included)—I somehow feel that something indefinable has passed me by. I am an outsider to the grand scheme of things.

I am alone.

Sure, I have friends, lots of them, and I have the Christmas cards to prove it, but most of them are raising families. They have real lives. I know I have a real life, too, but theirs seem realer. They have normal lives. I have a tour bus. Where is my wife? Where is my family? That's what we were all programmed for; how the fuck did I miss the programming. Where is my *really* real life?

The question rarely occurs to me, but at Christmastime it pounds relentlessly on my psyche, my conscience, and my frontal lobes. Or the back ones, I can never remember, because of all the pounding.

I dream of girlfriends past, of girlfriends present, and girlfriends future. It's as if I *am* Scrooge, but instead of being a miserly prick, I am emotionally withdrawn and inept at relationships, and the ghosts of my ex-girlfriends take me through our times together and remind me of the wondrous joys and warmth and fulfillment of the loves we shared. They then present to me a vision of the extraordinary children we would have had and how rich our family life together would have been. They then dance around me as achingly beautiful as I remember each of them as they sing like a chorus of angels, "Shithead. Shithead. Lew, you really stink. You have nothing left except your stinky stink."

And before I awaken, I am naked on a promontory as the wind howls and the vultures pick the meat off me. Needless to say, I awaken with a start.

Where did I go wrong?

Every Christmas I feel that I must now mate and have a family, or else all of my time on this planet has been for naught. I realize this is totally irrational, as if I am awash in the hormones produced by a romance novel or the film version of "The Gift of the Magi."

In the end, my Christmas is not about Christmas. It's about me. I spend it rattling down the corridors of my mind, jiggling the knobs on imaginary locked doors, behind which just might be all the answers I have spent a lifetime desperately searching for, wondering how I ended up becoming me. Just me. By myself. Alone.

Let me show you what I mean.

THANKSGIVING

❄

I hear the peaceful sounds of waves doing their dance on the beach as I bask in a sun that seems just a little too close to the earth today. Birds are twittering. (Birds twitter, humans shouldn't. Trust me, it's a law of nature—number 7, I think.) Occasionally I hear the piercing cry of a seabird that sits in a tree a few feet from my chaise lounge.

I am reading George Carlin's final book, *Last Words*. I am enjoying it. I am enjoying where I'm sitting, too. I am at peace. It's Thanksgiving and I am far away from home. Literally and figuratively.

I am in Costa Rica. That's right, you read that correctly. I was in Costa Rica during a major American holiday. What can I say? I'm a rebel. Besides, where else would one spend Thanksgiving?

But why Costa Rica, you ask? Why would I leave my native land as the days get shorter and shorter, the weather gets crummier and crummier, and the world gets crazier and crazier?

For years my friend Neil and I have chosen to leave the United States for an annual vacation. This all began about ten years ago, when we both realized we were raging workaholics and we desperately needed to set aside a few days each year to ensure that we got a break of some sort.

But why Thanksgiving, you ask? Isn't it the beginning of the holiday season? Isn't this the time to sit around the hearth (if one has a hearth) with one's family (if one has a family), in order to refresh the warmth of your blood ties and bonds?

Not if your mothers can't cook.

When your mother has no concept of how to cook a turkey, let alone the mashed potatoes, the stuffing, the gravy, the cranberry sauce, the green vegetables, the apple and the pumpkin pies, and as a kid you can see your folks hoping someone will invite your family over for Thanksgiving dinner so that your mother doesn't have to cook, you learn pretty quickly that at Thanksgiving, it's time to get the fuck out of Dodge.

I can remember the last Thanksgiving I spent in the United States. I went with Neil and his lovely wife, Laurie, who has since passed on, to have Thanksgiving dinner at Neil's parents' house. Neil always said that his mother could go head-to-head with mine in a gastronomic demolition derby. And he was right. Neil's mother prepared a meal that was just as unbelievable as my mother's cooking. I knew then that we were moments away from a reality show I'm sure would be a huge success. We could call it *WHAT THE FUCK AM I EATING?!* (Hey, if there's a show called *I Didn't Know I Was Pregnant*, or, as I like to call it, *Jesus Christ, Am I an Idiot or What?* then my cooking-show idea could certainly work.)

But back to the two mothers. That something potentially mouthwatering could be put in the oven and come out as the *illusion* of food is a trick few cooks can pull off. In short, Neil's mother and mine completely redefined the definition of cooking.

The joy of these kinds of meals—such as there is—is in the chewing. There is barely any taste. And aroma? Don't make me laugh. A turkey done until it has been sapped of any moisture, as if it was created from the dust of the Kalahari, has no scent to it at all.

It is as if killing the turkey the first time wasn't enough. Cooks of this particular caliber don't even want the memory of its potential deliciousness to linger. But at least the turkey didn't suffer alone—it had plenty of company. There were potatoes screaming for gravy that never made it to the table due to some hideous kitchen accident. And the green beans seemed to be weeping as if they wished to return to the field of their birth, hoping for a fresh start. In truth, I can't remember the rest of the meal; I believe I have repressed the memory of it. But Neil was right. His mother, in her own fashion, had created a meal that I thought only my mother could have laid waste to.

You hate to talk about your mothers' cooking this way, but it's this kind of consistently bad holiday cooking that made us flee the country on a national holiday, as if we were warned that we were about to be hit by a natural catastrophe, only ours was man-made and, disconcertingly, taking place in our mothers' kitchens.

But a twice-killed bird is not the only reason I have an aversion to what should be my day of thanks. As wonderful as so many find Christmas, it still hits us with the force of a hurricane, as it begins, with a vengeance, at Thanksgiving. And then there it is, twenty-four hours a day, as we are pounded relentlessly with music and advertising and everything that tradition and history and the media can throw at us.

Thanksgiving is the beginning of a relentless assault on our senses. To leave then and return after the high winds of marketing have begun to settle down just a little bit makes a lot of sense to me. As a bonus, the people around you have gotten over the initial trauma. So by going out of the country at Thanksgiving, you escape the first week of Christmas, which feels like a year by my calendar. And that only leaves you with another four years left before you finally stumble to the 25th of December.

Getting out of town at Thanksgiving makes Christmastime a hell of a lot easier for me.

So here I am in Central America, far from the maddening crowds. I lean back in my chair. I close my eyes and embrace the serenity. Yes, you heard me right—there is serenity. And tranquillity. And above all else, peace. Commodities I have so little of in my life. It takes me a while to get used to it, as at first it's a bit unsettling and unnerving, but I finally let myself go as the voices inside my skull drift into the sweet silence that envelops me.

And then, as the novelist Thomas Pynchon so aptly wrote, "A screaming comes across the sky." It pierces through the fragile sense of well-being that was nestling into me and rends the very fabric of existence with its insistent wail.

What is that ungodly and inhuman cacophony?

It's a child. A child whose lungs are bursting through its mouth in a cry of high-pitched demand and need not heard before in the history of the human species. And, no, it is not my inner child, which on occasion has been heard to wail in my soul like a banshee.

A KID! ARE YOU KIDDING ME?!!

We are in the middle of paradise. I'm just about to do something I have almost forgotten how to do—relax—

when out of the blue there appears this lovely, precious bundle of joy with a name like Tucker or Skip or Pip. Why is he screaming? What more can he need in life? Is the perfection that surrounds him not enough? Of course it isn't. What does he know of perfection? He's three years old, for fuck's sake. He has needs that perfection can't fulfill. This kid has deep-seated needs. He needs to know with absolute certainty that he has an effect on those around him. This is just one of the hundreds of tests that Pip must run daily so he can mature into the kind of human being who will enjoy and appreciate this heaven on earth.

WHEN HE IS FUCKING OLD ENOUGH TO ENJOY IT!

Well, apparently, that's not going to happen in the next five minutes. So for God's sake, would one of his parents get him a milkshake, a fluffy towel, a sleeping pill, whatever—anything to shut him the fuck up, he's killing my sense of bliss. And I rarely if ever feel bliss, or what I think bliss is.

Then I look around. Jesus Christ, this joint is crawling with kids. You've got to be kidding me. This has got to be some grand cosmic joke. Someone has got to be laughing about this somewhere in the Universe, and that someone doesn't seem to give a shit about me.

It took me my entire life to be able to afford to come to a place like this and also not feel guilty about doing so. At long last, I've found someplace where I could rest my weary bones before returning to the madness. I am extraordinarily blessed to be here. And I know it.

But does that three-year-old actually need to take time off? And if so, from what, pray tell? Potty training? Was Pip seeking solitude, a haven from the insanity of life in playgroup back in the U.S.? Was his anguish at home so deep that, frothing at the mouth, he threw a fit so violent that the kitty ended up dead in the toilet, its fur ripped from its body? Did his parents at that point turn to each other and sigh: "I don't think that the counseling is really doing the job for our little darling. It doesn't seem to be spot-on. Forget the experts, I think what Pip really needs is a tropical vacation."

And unfortunately, it's not just Pip. There are kids of every size, shape, and description crawling all over the place. With nannies akimbo. And what is that in the little bundle? Is it . . . ? OH, FOR GOD'S SAKE! INFANTS! They've even brought infants. To what end? For what purpose? WHY? By gracing you with that precious gift, wasn't God sending you a deeper message? Were these parents not listening when God proclaimed to the newborn and his family: "For every season there is a purpose, and now is the time for you to nurture your little baby in a little bubble of love of your own creation in the house where you have chosen to live, in order for that baby not to have to undergo the horrifying vagaries of aircraft cabin pressure at 35,000 feet, which can wreak such havoc on his barely formed inner ears"?

Let me see if I can put it more succinctly: STAY HOME, IDIOTS!

And did these people ever consider what a tropical climate might do to their baby? (A baby that has barely adjusted to the climate of his or her own hometown, I might add.) Have these parents no fear that their pride and joy might contract some sort of inscrutable and incurable skin rash? I know that I'm worried about waking up to find my body covered with red splotches outlined in white with a star in the middle. I don't know what it might be, but I know it's serious. If *I'm* scared, shouldn't these parents fear for the well-being of their darlings, too?

Of course they should. But they're too busy sunning themselves near the pool while playing the latest app on their iPhone to realize this.

Some might say I am overreacting, that I am being overprotective of the infant. Bullshit. I'm not. I'm being overprotective of *myself*. I don't want babies on my vacation. Besides, it's Thanksgiving. Shouldn't they all be at home, where they belong? For God's sake, it's the beginning of the holiday season. Where are these families' family values?

A child needs memories of the family together as Dad slices the turkey, their brothers and sisters arguing spiritedly about who gets the remote control during the Macy's Thanksgiving Day parade, their uncles snoring through the football games as their aunts gossip after dinner. They need to witness the alcohol, the rage, the tears of regret—things that can sink deeply into their barely formed psyches and scar them forever. Otherwise what are they going to talk to their shrink about?

Trust me, I know what I'm talking about. Since my family rarely celebrated our own Thanksgiving, I am nearly bereft of family values of any sort. But that's a whole other set of problems and a whole other book.

But there are little tics I have because of Thanksgivings I spent with other families when I was growing up. For example, I weep whenever anyone brings out a gravy boat with real gravy. Or I hear angry screams whenever I see a bottle of Old Crow bourbon.

The only good thing one can say about giving a child who can barely speak a Thanksgiving in a tropical resort is that it's not an Al-Qaeda Thanksgiving. There's no chance the kids will ask, "Daddy, why is the turkey ticking?"

When the children aren't going off half-cocked outdoors, they are going off half-cocked indoors. I sadly learn there is no separate dining room for them. From the breakfast buffet to fine dining at dinner, the kids are flittering around the place, or staring blankly at their portobello mushroom quiches with Gruyère and crab just before they burst into tears and begin shrieking that they hate it. They even have their own breakfast buffet line where they can be assured of mainlining enough sugar to keep them rocketing through space till the sun goes down.

Even though I hate to swim, I tried going to the adult pool to escape the madness and calm my nerves. Unfortunately, I discovered that the adult pool was much smaller than the main pool, and that only fueled my rage. Is this a joke? As a kid, I always got the fucking small pool, the wading pool in the backyard. And now as an adult I still get the small pool, while the kids get the big pool.

WHY, THOSE LITTLE FUCKERS, IT'S JUST NOT RIGHT!

To me, this hotel has to be a place for adults and maybe, just maybe—and *very* grudgingly—teenagers. But children? NOOOOOOOO! It's for romantic getaways, or to just get away from it all. And the "all" in "getting away from it all" definitely includes children, who, I REPEAT, don't need to get away from anything.

If these parents can afford an overpriced vacation for themselves and their four children and the nanny during the holidays, maybe they could put their money to better use. How about paying more taxes? Maybe their taxes need to be raised a little. Is this why we refuse to raise taxes on the wealthy? So they have enough money to let their bratty little kids soak up the Costa Rican sun? Really? Fuck them.

Too harsh, you think? So, we all should just say:

"Fuck the infrastructure"? "Fuck the returning soldier"? "Fuck the emergency we can't imagine. Just pass the tanning butter"? I say fuck that.

I can hear you now: "But, Lewis, you're enjoying a vacation, too. Aren't you lounging in the tropical sun?"

I know, I know. And I admit I feel a little guilty about being here by myself. But I also think that the government needs to raise my taxes so I don't go to these places and therefore don't feel guilty.

All I'm saying is at times like these, you can tax the rich a little more.

Don't cry. I said *a little*. God knows you wouldn't want to take too much from the rich because even though they'd still be rich, they wouldn't be *as* rich. And maybe they'd have to stay home at Thanksgiving with the kids, instead of unleashing them on me.

Look, I don't mean to be unduly rude, but I have to be. I have been left with no choice. Thanksgiving isn't a family time for me—so much so that I literally flee the country. And I really, *really* don't want to spend my few days of peace with yours.

This type of holiday family gathering at a tropical resort was once the province of only the superrich. We are talking the Astors. The Fricks. The Kennedys, the Fords, the Hoodahaddahs, and the Honorable Their-ShitNeverSmells. All the big families of note.

The reason they went off for the holidays was so that they could all gather together and count their money with families of like social status and make sure they married within their class, their very upper upper class. This assured that they kept all the money to themselves. These vacations were a way to introduce their children to the entitlement they felt they so richly deserved.

Okay, maybe I exaggerate here, but just a little.

But these kids in Costa Rica with me are not Fricks or Fords or Hoodahaddahs. And as they sit on the beach before me, taking a vacation like this, sucking on the little coconut-mango smoothies the hotel staff passes around when the sun is at its peak, I can't help wondering what this kind of extraordinary experience is going to do to their young minds. What the fuck are they going to expect as adults?

I understand it's not their fault that their parents are wealthy, self-indulgent idiots who don't want their child suffering the indignities of a Holiday Inn off the interstate the way they had to when they were kids.

So when I look at the children frolicking in the spectacularly blue ocean in front of me, I am not looking at America's future. I am seeing tomorrow's basket cases, the people who'll have changed their names to Tush-Tush or Kumsquatch or Poached in order to stand out from the crowd and who will never be noticed for their talents or accomplishments but for their massively narcissistic egos. I am looking at the next generation's Paris Hiltons and Kardashian kids and the motley collection of morons from whatever new reality shows are going to induce nausea in me in the future.

Of course, every one of these kids scampering across the sandy beach won't end up like them, but I can guarantee that a lot of them will. We are spawning another generation that feels that the world around them exists only for the sake of their own egos. Egos that grow like a rapidly advancing cancer, that will engulf and consume us in whatever medium is the next carrier of the images that surround us. These are the egos that will create tomorrow's world; and, sadly, these are the egos that will believe they are more important than the world in which they exist.

"Jesus, that's bleak," you think. "It can't be that bad, Lewis. Besides, who are you to be standing in judgment of these people?"

I take your point. I am down here among the privileged during the worst economic downturn of my lifetime. I'm the little pig going back for the third time to the breakfast buffet while many of my countrymen are going without breakfast at all. I am screaming about these kids but, truth be told, I am the irresponsible one in this whole scenario.

I am the one who should know better. I should be out with Habitat for Humanity, only I am worthless with tools. But I should at least be putting my money where my mouth is. Okay, I admit it. I am a piece of shit.

But I am a piece of shit trying to relax on a beach. I don't need these kinds of thoughts racing through my brain while I am supposed to be *on vacation.* I will be home soon enough, where I can properly berate and loathe myself in the quiet solitude of my own apartment.

So thank God I have more than one voice in my head. There is another country to be heard from. Forget about tomorrow, Lewis, you've got some sort of native rum concoction in front of you, and there are the notes of some Costa Rican love song lingering in the air. You're not standing knee-deep in the rising tide of the Christmas onslaught. And you deserve a rest, that's why you are having these crazy thoughts. Really, everything is going to be just fine. Just the way God and your accountant planned it.

God, what is that? Is that a retching sound I hear? Oh Jesus, little Pip is throwing up. Too much sun, I guess.

I can hear my shrink now: "And when did you lose your ability to empathize with others, Lewis?"

"Oh, this past Thanksgiving," I will reply.

"Do you want to talk about it?"

"I'm not ready. I'm still enjoying it."

I turn to Neil and his wife, Machiko (he has remarried and now the three of us go on these trips together). "It's been a great vacation," I say. I almost believe it. "We leave tomorrow and I haven't been upgraded to first class. But I can handle it. Unless Pip is sitting in a first-class seat."

And of course he was. You know what a three-year-old needs most is ample legroom and free cocktails. To me he's a little shit, and it's not even his fault. It's mine.

It was a long trip. I took a short nap. We landed. We went through immigration. I was home.

And the Christmas season had arrived.

With a vengeance.

I was ready for it. I had girded my loins through epic battles with Pip. I would let the Christmas madness pass over me like all of those warm Costa Rican breezes.

And I didn't miss the turkey dinner. It was easier to handle Pip than my mother's Thanksgiving meal. Pip had also taught me an important lesson. I learned maybe it was a good thing I didn't have any children. And the no-kids thing certainly cuts down on my Christmas shopping.

THE HOOKER AT
ROCKEFELLER CENTER

❄

It is as hard for me to escape the Christmas season as it is for me to forget about sex. I mean, it does seem to me that popular culture and advertising spend an awful lot of time and money to remind my psyche that the season of Santa is upon me every year. Those same forces spend the same time and money talking to my penis. Between the two, my penis listens more often. Let's face it, if it's not the display of boobage in order to entice me toward drinking a certain beer, it's the boner pills, the hair gel, or body spray that gets you laid. And all these messages are transmitted before I even make it to my morning coffee. So while my penis pays close attention to everything, my psyche sometimes wanders. It's a problem I'm dealing with. But whenever I actually forget for a few moments that it's Christmastime, the tree at Rockefeller Center, much like a hooker working her favorite spot, is there to remind me.

I admit that there is something magical about a Christmas tree all dazzled up in lights. It's almost as breathtaking as a hooker gone wild in spangles. It gets to me. Maybe it's just that having a Christmas tree makes a living room just a little cozier. But I think it goes deeper than that. Maybe it's the sense of rebirth that the lights give to a very dead (or very artificial) tree. In the midst of winter, when a pall hangs heavy in the frozen gray air, these glittering reminders of holiday cheer can be downright comforting. I have to say, the same can be said about a hooker.

But—and this is very important—Christmas trees in Los Angeles, San Diego, Miami, or any warm climate always seem a bit weird to me—the veritable tits on a bull. Somehow they just don't belong. I suppose it works if you're raised in that climate, but for me, seeing a Christmas tree in sunny weather only makes me pine for winter. And as much as I hate winter—let me count the fucking ways—I'd rather experience it than pine for it.

I've got to admit, though, that during the times in my life when I've lived with people who had to have a Christmas tree, my Jewish upbringing left me ambivalent about it. My parents didn't go for Chanukah with a Christmas tree. No way. And I never understood the whole idea behind that combination. You do one holiday or the other, *not* both. Together they have no meaning.

It's like drinking Red Bull and vodka together. As I learned the hard way, whatever comes out of your mouth is loud and stupid.

To me, a tree during Chanukah was an interloper. I may like the way Christmas trees look when I drive by houses and see them in people's living rooms, with their twinkling lights aglow, I just don't want one. If ever I was stupid enough to put one up at my place, I know it would stand there, taunting me, saying: "What are you doing here, Jewboy?! This is *my* house. Jews don't have Christmas trees. Why don't you go to the temple and find a menorah to hang out with?" I don't need that kind of aggravation from a conifer.

There is one tree, though, that doesn't inspire any good feelings in me. In fact, it inspires rage. It's the tree that somebody—I still don't know who—puts up just after Thanksgiving at Rockefeller Center, right in the aorta of New York City. It makes me insane every year because it creates a bottleneck of epic proportions. Every artery of movement around it is clogged with too many people and too many cars, desperate to be in its presence. It's as if Jesus had set up shop on the skating rink below the tree and was doing a few heavenly triple lutzes to the delight of the masses.

Look, I live in New York. I have work to do here. I have people to see. I have to get around. I don't need this vast parade of humanity mowing me down to see a huge overdecorated Christmas tree, especially when I am actually at home for only a few weeks a year.

But nobody cares. Instead, each and every year the geniuses at Rockefeller Center cut down a tree, drive it into midtown, doll it up, and plunge it like a stake right into the heart of the city.

It isn't New Yorkers who go to see the tree. Noooooooooooo. It's tourists, out-of-towners from every corner of the United States and the world, from every imaginable place where they see fucking trees every fucking day of their lives. In their desperate need to see yet another tree, they make the life of this New Yorker impossible.

And here's the worst part of the whole thing. They come to New York in droves to see the same tree that they saw Al Roker light on television. It's the same fucking tree! These idiots already saw it from the comfort of their living rooms, where their own trees are twinkling. And if they think that weeks later Al Roker will still be standing next to that tree, waiting to greet them, they're fucking delusional. He's probably got a life.

If I had any guts I'd take a chain saw to the tree. But I'm sure it would be seen as a terrorist act. More likely I'd lose a hand in the process. So I'll have to be wilier. I'll have to use my brains instead. I think we should get the tree out of Manhattan and put it in the Bronx, Brooklyn, or Queens. People want to see a tree so bad, let them chase it, the fuckers. Staten Island would be a perfect spot. Let's see if they can find it among thousands of other trees.

Is the tree you have in your living room not enough for you? Then do a better job of decorating it and you won't need to put one up on the sidewalks I need to walk on. And if that doesn't satisfy you, find a hooker in an elf costume with lots of spangles.

CHRISTMAS MORNING

The Sun Rises on Our Hapless but (Somewhat) Hopeful Hero

❄

I wake up slowly. It is Christmas morning. When I turn in the bed, there is no one else, just an empty pillow. It is quiet. There are no delighted squeals of children in my living room. No lovely wife calling my name out in a tremolo for me to join them to open presents.

I am alone.

I never feel more alone than I do when I lie there in the stillness of another Christmas morning. When I was younger, being alone never really bothered me, as I always thought I would be married someday and there might even be children.

Although when it comes to children, I have never been absolutely certain that I wanted to be a father. I didn't have what seemed the natural desire to be a parent that many of my friends seemed to possess. I have never uttered the words "I can't wait to be a father." I've heard my friends say it. And I've always wondered how they knew that's what they wanted to be. I sure didn't.

I knew other things, of course. That I wanted to be a playwright, for one.

So why didn't I feel as strongly about having children? It was certainly easier to have a kid than to become a successful writer. I wrote and I wrote and I wrote but nobody seemed interested in what I had to say. The world doesn't really want a lot of playwrights—certainly less than they seem to want other types of writers. I couldn't even get a teaching job with a Master of Fine Arts in Playwriting. By the time you finish saying it, you're broke. Crack whores make more money than playwrights, and they have a driving incentive to keep at it because of their addiction.

I always thought that I wanted to have a real income before I was going to think about having children. Granted, if everyone in this country shared my philosophy, we'd have a lot less children. Which might not be so bad, considering how many miserable people with miserable kids there are out there. These families spring up all over the place because there's an insane notion in this country that if you have a child, everything will work itself out for everybody. We will just do what we want to and God will provide. I have never understood this notion, and I have watched families live tortured lives because of it. It's on the back of this kind of wishful thinking that Wal-Mart made its fortune.

I have had a lot of primal urges (and I will keep those to myself, thank you very much), but I have never felt the biological urge to have a child. Or is it biological need? Or biological drive? Whatever it is, I don't have it. (I never felt there was a necessity for me to contribute to the survival of the species.) My parents weren't even that interested in having grandchildren. As my mother once so sweetly put it: "You and your brother were enough. Do I really need more of the same? Are you serious?"

If that didn't upset you, my mother also said, over a lunch recently in Las Vegas, "Ronnie [my brother] and you weren't my idea. They were his." Then she pointed to my father. "If it were up to me, we wouldn't have had kids. But he was keen on it." And then she said, "I guess that's not something you tell your child."

No shit. It's a good thing Mom waited till I was sixty to break the news. If she told me when I was ten, I would no doubt have spent my life on a respirator.

Maybe that's why I don't have those paternal feelings.

Or maybe it's got more to do with the extremely bad marriage I had.

To put it in the simplest of terms: At twenty-six I married a woman I had been living with for a couple of years. She was pregnant. Five months after the birth of the son that I thought was mine, she announced that it wasn't. It turns out while we were living together she was seeing another guy. Even though it was more than likely that the other guy was the father, she said that I was, because I was going to the Yale School of Drama at the time. See how an Ivy League education pays off? (The other guy was not only an actor, he was a *mime*. I have always had an instinctive aversion to mimes. That was when I figured out why.)

Wow, you say.

Holy fuck, I said.

And then I went to the ICU, the one that exists in my head.

Where was Maury Povich, the man who has made his living off of figuring out who's the babydaddy, when I needed him? (By the way, "babydaddy" is an expression as juvenile as those who use the word. If you use the word you shouldn't be allowed to have a child, or even babysit.)

I had no idea a woman would even think of doing something like this. Seriously, I didn't. Do the words "young and stupid" mean anything to you?

This was all pre–Oprah and Dr. Phil, of course. Until they showed up, I labored under the delusion that the middle class was insulated from this kind of nonsense. How would I have even heard about incest if it weren't for these two? Who knew there was so much of it? What the fuck is the matter with us?

"But you're avoiding the subject, Lewis. Give us the details of your sad story."

Why should I? Aren't the simple bare-naked facts enough?

Enough is never enough in this culture. There always has to be more. It's why we're spiritually thin and physically fat. It wasn't enough that Kate and Jon Gosselin were a reality show. When it went off the air and the world heaved a collective sigh of relief, we still needed them to become news because there has to be more. It's why we slow down to see the smashed car at the side of the road. "Were they organ donors?" we might think as we crane our necks to gaze at the wreckage. "Where's the blood? What do you suppose their blood types were?"

And speaking of blood, that's how I found out the apple of my eye was without any of my seeds. I thought we should find out who the biological father was if we could. It seemed like the responsible thing to do, since I wasn't going to take my wife's word for it. This was before DNA testing, so the chances of discovering who the father was were slim at best—a 29 percent chance, as a matter of fact. You could only figure it out from the blood types.

There we all were. Alleged dad 1 (me), alleged dad 2 (the mime), mom, and son, waiting in the doctor's office together for the nurse to take our blood. The kid was screaming. I don't think it was just about the nurse drawing his blood.

The kid was always screaming. *Always*. He had colic. So did I when I was a kid. I used to think that maybe it was genetic, but in this instance obviously that wasn't the case. Wasn't it enough that he wasn't my kid? Did he really need to have colic, too?

Now that I think about it, maybe he knew we didn't share any genetic markers and that's why he was screaming. Perhaps he was screaming at me: "Get out before it's too late! I'm not yours—get out now!"

Boy, that kid could wail. I used to spend eight hours a day with him by myself, as my then-wife had a job in the afternoons and the evenings and I was working in the mornings, writing a play—with kids, for other kids. I spent all morning with kids and then came home to a baby I thought was my little boy.

Before I go any further, I have to say this: Parents, especially moms, who spend most of their day with an infant have my undying respect. It can be a lonely, completely brutal experience, as you make every attempt to stop the baby's tears and *every single thing that you try FAILS!* Gently rocking the bed, swinging them in their little swing, holding them close, driving them around in the car, or singing a lullaby has no effect on them. It only seems to feed their need to scream louder. Vainly I'd scream back at him. The shrieks and the cries crush your fragile ego's need to help and eventually you just can't take it anymore as the crying and the fussing grind on day after day after day. Bundle of joy, my ass! Being the parent of a newborn is fucking hard work.

I am now going to say something horrible. I know it's horrible because you're not supposed to say it. I know it, and so will you. I know I shouldn't say it, and you know I shouldn't say it. It upsets people, because they will completely misconstrue your intention for saying it. But here it is:

Having spent as much time as I have with a colicky baby, I am not so quick to judge a young mother who might snap and somehow hurt or even kill her child.

It's wrong. I know it's wrong. I am not a monster. And I'm not saying it isn't wrong.

Let me repeat myself: IT'S WRONNNNNNNN-GGGGG!

But I was a well-educated twenty-six-year-old who certainly had a grasp of right and wrong. And I had help: when my wife came home from work, she took over the primary care of the baby. But we all know from reading the papers that there are young single moms who find themselves trapped with an infant who is breaking them. And after hours and hours and hours, where there is no escape for them, some of them snap.

It's not right. I know that, and so do you. But I just have a small understanding of how it *could* happen. And it's a tragedy.

One thing I did notice about myself in my brief stint

at child-rearing is that I never developed any real communication skills with the infant—or with any infant, for that matter. I felt like an utter idiot when I gee-geed or gaa-gaaed or goo-gooed. "Did you see the itty butterfly? Pretty. The itty-bitty pretty butterfly. Did you?" Of course he didn't. HE WAS TOO BUSY BAWLING HIS EYES OUT!

Sorry. I know it's probably the right thing to do, to talk to a baby as if he can actually understand you, I just wasn't any good at it. I'd talk to the kid, but I was never fully committed to it. And I knew he wasn't really listening. I have the same problem today when I try to talk to God.

Coincidence? You tell me.

We can move on now.

I am sure that this experience has a lot to do with the way I view parenthood today. The first shrink I spent time with after the blood tests came back and the dust settled and I knew I wasn't a father, said I'd never get over it. That wasn't good news. And it certainly didn't help to know that. I just really wanted to know how I could ever trust my taste in women again. So I was looking for a little more encouragement—or at least a bit of positive bullshit—from someone who was actually getting paid to help me. (And shouldn't that be a course for shrinks before they graduate? Better Bullshit 101? It might be the most useful course future psychiatrists could ever take.)

The fact still remained that until I did (as they so insanely put it) "the right thing" and married my pregnant girlfriend, parenthood wasn't at the top of my list of goals for my life.

And what exactly is "the right thing"? And for whom exactly is it "right"? Her? Maybe. The baby? For a while. Me? Not so much. I guess two out of three means you've got a winner. I would love to know how successful doing "the right thing" has been across the centuries. Are there any stats on this? Maybe the "right thing" isn't so right. There's a reason they call it a shotgun wedding. Someone is taking a bullet, for sure. It could be the mom, the pop, or the baby, or any combo platter.

One thing I do know is I don't believe in "the right thing" anymore. You do the thing where the least amount of damage is inflicted on that helpless infant. And getting married may be the worst thing you can do.

But then again, you can understand, I am a little jaded.

And so I lie there in my warm bed, on a day that I don't really celebrate, and I feel alone. "Where is my lovely wife and my adoring children?" I think. Have I made a horrible mistake? Have I taken the wrong path in the Robert Frost poem? Two roads diverged in a yellow wood? And what the fuck does "diverged" mean? Will I never know these great joys of life? Is it too late?

"Nonsense, Lewis," I think. "You're still young by

today's standards. You can do it. You don't have to be alone. All you've got to do, Lewis, is fall in love, get married, and have a child, so by the time you're seventy-five you can play catch with him. So that when you miss the kid's fastball and it drills into your chest, crushing your sternum and throwing you against the metal patio furniture, shattering your pelvis, you can die happily, content in the knowledge that you were a family man."

No thanks.

I hate this feeling, and yet every Christmas I slowly allow myself to sink into it. I can't fight it. It envelops me like some melancholy marshmallow. It's more comfortable than thinking about the steps that have brought me to this moment in time. Quite simply, I've given up a real life for a career in show business. What the fuck is the matter with me? My friends have careers. They have children. They are wives and husbands. They have LIVES! I have no wife, no kids, no backyard, no minivan—but I have two bathrooms, by God. And they are fucking mechanical marvels of design and efficiency. (What more could a single man ask for than a bathroom to shower in and a bathroom to take a bath in?)

My friends were no more prepared for parenthood than I was. They're not any brighter or dumber than me. They're not nicer—well, maybe a little nicer. God knows their sperm isn't in better shape. In all honesty, I thought every one of their kids would be born with a helmet. Which says more about my friends' younger days than it does about the terrific kids they sired.

(The last line, for those of you who immediately got upset by such a reference to the mentally challenged, should realize, or at least try to fathom, that this is a joke about my friends' *sperm*. You can be upset about a sperm joke. I can understand that. But people have got to cease and desist from judging jokes when they don't get the joke just because they are worried about the etiquette of the joke. This joke has "etiquette" written all over it. If you are reading this book and have gotten to this page and this joke has upset you, there is something deeply wrong with you. Just because it ends with the image of a helmet doesn't mean that's what the joke is about. SO GET WITH THE PROGRAM! Okay, let's move on.)

Wait a minute. Good God, I am divorced. Isn't there a statute of limitations on divorce? Especially if it was granted more than twenty years ago. For crying out loud, if you're divorced and you get remarried, you don't have to check both the married *and* divorced boxes, so why shouldn't I be able to just check the single box, rather than confront the ashes of my mistake?

Single at sixty-one. Do people think I'm gay? Am I? Uh . . . no.

I do not wake up on Christmas morning and lie around in bed and question my sexuality. I've always known I am straight. Probably too straight. That's probably how you end up single at my age. You worship women, as in making them so important to you that you forget about yourself and so you devote your life to finding just the right one for yourself, and when you do, because you've been so blind in your worship, you end up marrying a woman who is having another man's baby.

(TIME OUT! My editor thinks what I have here is "too discursive." Well, Christmas makes me fucking discursive. It starts me thinking about stuff Christians don't think about at Christmas, 'cause it's fucking Christmas for them.)

And while we're on the subject of straight: How is it that so many straight people who are so absolutely certain of their straightness cannot comprehend that someone can be absolutely sure they are gay? In a world awash in heterosexual pornography, a part of our population remains unmoved by it. And there's a reason. They are not heterosexual. That doesn't make them scary. It just makes them gay.

And enough already with the "Don't ask, don't tell" happy horseshit. Gays didn't need to ask if they were gay. God told them. And if God told them, that's all you need to know, 'cause He's God and He wouldn't have made people gay unless He thought it was right. How do I know this? Because He's God and He's smarter than you. He also figured He didn't need to write more than two books because He thought since we were made in His own image, that we would be smarter. So in a way, you let Him down. But what else is new?

And if you don't like what I just said, tough. That's the God I believe in and that's the way He thinks. Maybe your God will have some thoughts someday.

But what do I know? I don't have a family, so who am I to be making light of your family values. And since I don't have a family, I don't get it, do I?

So as I lie there, supine, pondering my failure to create a life beyond my own, yelling at the world around me, I wonder how do I prevent myself from wallowing in a stew of self-pity. What should I do? I need catharsis. Do I weep copious tears? Do I induce electroshock with a hair dryer in the shower? Do I go online and find a Russian mail-order bride with a baby?

No.

I lay there, snug in my bed, and wonder what the fuck Santa got me for Christmas. For starters, I hope I get an at-home DNA kit. I am definitely never going through that shit again.

IT IS BETTER TO ~~GUILT~~ GIVE . . .

❄

I've always been deeply impressed by the way you Christians pour it on at Christmas. It may have all started with a little incense and myrrh, but you took that basic idea and went apeshit with it. Everybody gets tons of presents: boxes from one end of the house to the other, enough to shelter an entire homeless village. All festooned (this is the only time you'd ever think of using that word) in paper of every imaginable color, with rainbows of ribbon and bows bedecking them. If that weren't enough, you stuff stockings with even more gifts, from chocolates to penknives. (I could never get my parents to buy me a penknife.) Everybody no doubt even wakes up with a little gift in their ass; you people just haven't told us Jews about that.

At Chanukah we get nothing. We don't even get

stockings. At my house we got socks, and they were irregulars, which figures. It's supposed to be the Festival of Lights, but it wasn't really that festive, not compared to how you Christians carry on. Let's face it, eight little candles do not a spectacular light show make.

Is it better to give than to receive? Well, if you are really, *really* going to be honest, nothing beats getting stuff. Just watch the faces of those going through the goody bags after a benefit and you'll see what I mean. These bags are filled with all sorts of items, donated by companies and individuals, as a reward for those people who came out and supported the charity, attended the opening, or sat through the awards show. People who have everything, who can buy and sell you and me and still have enough left over for a beach house and a couple of sports cars, shove their heads deep into these goody bags, hoping to find some spectacular geegaw they don't have already. And even if they do have it, they're greedy enough to be thrilled to have another one just like it. As George Carlin put it so beautifully, "People like their stuff." Amen to that.

I can't even begin to imagine what Christmas shopping must be like for you people. I mean, sure I shop, but not the way you guys do it. I walk into a couple of stores, buy my friends gifts I think they'll like, and walk out. Done. For those of you who really celebrate Christmas, the shopping for it must be hell. Pounded insensate for weeks by a series of ads *demanding* that you shop,

but never really having the time to really do it properly—
by that I mean rationally—and then rushing to sit
around with family and relations for one morning, rip-
ping open gifts like maniacs, while everyone around you
is judging the gifts that you gave. They can see who you
like more. You've given them a concrete expression of
your feelings. Now, that's not just pressure, that's a
nightmare.

In all honesty, I have never understood why you
Christians shop before Christmas at all. It's when all the
stuff is at its most expensive, except that first Black Fri-
day where there are some deals that turn crowds nearly
suicidal—and most definitely homicidal—in their lust
for the great buy. So why don't you folks wait till the
26th of December, when things are the cheapest? Just a
small suggestion, from a Jew who has your best interests
at heart.

I think the real joy of getting the gift is not the gift
itself, it's tearing off the wrapping paper, because until
the present is actually opened, there could be anything
under that paper. *Anything.* The mind runs wild with
anticipation. Is it going to be extraordinary stocks and
bonds worth millions? Is it a series of erotic photos that
are actually erotic? Or is it something that I truly wanted
that will make my life complete?

SON OF A BITCH . . . COULD IT BE THE MEAN-
ING OF LIFE ITSELF?

Of course it never is, but looking down at that present

as you almost burst in expectation, there's that brief moment where you're full of hope.

And more often than not it's a massive disappointment, because you don't even know what it is, or what it could possibly be used for.

"Now, *this* is really something," you say.

"It certainly is, and it's one of a kind," the giver says. "It's a Hiccup-stopper. The instructions are on the back."

"Wow, really, it stops hiccups . . ."

"That's what it says. I saw it on TV. You've got to be careful with it or you could choke to death, but it stopped that guy's hiccups just like that. A few more inventions like this and our economy will be up and humming again."

"It's made in China."

"Yeah, but it was our idea."

The only joy that kind of gift gives comes from trying to figure out why someone invented it in the first place and why, in the second place, someone who claims actually to like you would buy it for you.

You do get jazzed, though, when you find the absolutely perfect gift for the absolutely right person. Like the time I found a duck-hunting rifle for Dick Cheney. It's a pleasure because it almost never happens, because you are usually so fucking busy and everything is so last-minute.

"Are you sure you don't have this in blue?"

"I'm sorry, but this was a very big seller. This is all we have left."

"It's perfect, except for the color. I've never seen that color before. And I think I know why. It's hideous."

"They call it Mucus. And it's very hip."

"No one is that hip."

"Well, maybe you shouldn't wait till the night before Christmas to do your shopping."

The one time I truly feel happy about giving a gift is when I am writing a check to a nonprofit organization or a charity. I've spent most of my life begging and borrowing to get by, so when I actually started to make enough money to actually have to file a tax return—and there were years when I didn't have to, believe me; the IRS would just call to see if I was still breathing—it was nice to be able to pass on some of my good fortune. When I finally had enough money to do this, I was thrilled to be able to give to all of those people who needed it, and those who do so much good for others, those who've actually devoted themselves to the welfare of humanity. It made me feel that at least I was helping somehow, instead of just taking up space. As much as people talk about how important comedy is in their lives, it's not really comparable to what those people do who are working their asses off to make this world truly a better place. We comics basically come in to wax the floors and wash the windows after all of the really hard work is done.

So every Christmas morning when I get up, I start my true Christmas ritual.

I roll out of bed, put on the coffee, and grab my checkbook and the stack of letters appealing to me for whatever donation I can make, and sit down at the table. I go through these pleas, one at a time, and write checks. And I give to a wide variety of organizations—as wide as I can think. The checks aren't as big as they probably should be, as I still live in fear that someone will see through me and my house of cards will crumble and I'll be shit out of luck and money. Then I'll have to go to a few of these groups and ask for their help. My life always seems to be moments away from being ironic.

The physical act of writing these checks and putting stamps on the envelopes and licking them shut—and remembering to include the fucking check—makes me feel wonderful, like I'm part of something, like I'm *helping*. I may not have a family of my own, but, goddamnit, I can help somebody else's.

By doing this, I have left myself open to a constant stream of additional appeals from the very groups I have given to, along with crap of every size, shape, and description that these organizations feel obligated to send along as a thank-you gift they think might grab my attention and make me want to send them more money. Don't they get it? I am sending them money to do good things, not so they can send me tchotchkes that I then have to feel guilty about throwing out. How much money are they pissing away on mailing costs? And manpower? And energy? It drives me insane.

And there doesn't seem to be any way to stop them. I have tried. Oh, God, how I've tried. But no one cares. The organizations think it's a good idea. It's not. They are just trying to make me feel guilty all year round. (By the way, Mr. Black, that keychain you just threw away was made especially for you by the starving kids and their starving parents.) I don't need their help. I can muster up guilt all on my own, thank you very much. I am a Jew, as anybody who's been paying attention here will recall. When it comes to that sort of thing, we are professionals.

I also feel a bit guilty while I write those checks as I try to figure out which organization do I give more to. I always start with the United Negro College Fund, because of former vice president Dan Quayle's immortal screw-up.

Do you remember that? No, I didn't think so. Well, let me remind you.

Back when he was vice president, Quayle addressed the United Negro College Fund, whose slogan is "A mind is a terrible thing to waste." Well, this genius said, *when he was standing in front of the group and speaking to its members*: "You take the UNCF model, that what a waste it is to lose one's mind or not to have a mind is being very wasteful . . ." And could anyone be a better example of that than you, Mr. Vice President?

(I quote him to remind you, and myself, that anyone can be vice president. *Anyone.* And that's not necessarily a good thing.)

From there on, it's organizations of every size, shape, and description. Those who help the homeless, food banks, emergency relief funds, all sorts of groups of doctors, those helping minorities who are getting screwed, nonprofit theaters, legal aid and lawyers working for hopeless causes that shouldn't be hopeless causes, educational outfits, kids' groups, environmentalists, anyone who wants to make a more peaceful world, anyone fighting idiots in power, and anyone trying to find a cure for diseases. Especially those diseases that have either stricken friends of mine or taken their lives. Then it's diseases that I'm afraid *I* am going to get. And I am afraid I am going to get all of them, even juvenile diseases I am far too old to possibly get. And I am afraid I am going to die from all of them.

I do not tell you this to show what a good boy I am. Not in the least. Because I know I'm not. I don't even get carpal tunnel syndrome while doing this. I never do enough. Never. No one can. And yet, oddly enough, on every Christmas morning, this makes me happy.

It's the best present I give myself every year.[*] (In fact, it's the only time I give the absolutely perfect present to the absolutely right person.)

---

[*]This chapter was written with a pen provided by the National Shingles Foundation.

CHRISTMAS DAY, 11:07 A.M.

Dashing Through the Shower,
Losing My Mind Along the Way

❄

After I've written the last check, I wonder why there isn't some major nonprofit scientific research organization experimenting with creating replaceable human organs, so one doesn't have to wait around for some horrifying traffic accident in order to receive a new liver or lung or heart. We don't need to be able to download phone applications, we need to find a way to download organs. And quickly, as I don't know how much longer mine are going to be in running order. Fucking mortality makes you think about this shit. I'd replace all of my organs now if I could. Actually, if at all possible, I'd replace them every three years, because you can't really do all that much damage in only three years and then you'd be starting fresh again. Nothing I'd like better than to stave off my inevitable demise.

It then occurs to me that if I had done all of these donations with a credit card, I could have accrued points with my giving. I could have been giving and receiving at the same time. Talk about multitasking. And if I had been doing this for years I could have saved up enough points so I wouldn't have to pay for my new organs.

But I know I'd feel guilty about having gotten something in return for my charitable contribution. Probably more than the folks getting the charity. As if I'm not blessed enough to be in a position to help out, even in a small way.

What kind of greedy little pig have I become? What kind of greedy little pigs have so many of us become?

It's truly shocking that we reward those in our culture who already have too much as it is. And that there are folks for whom there is no such thing as having too much. They believe that having too much—everything they ever want every moment of their lives—is their birthright. And it's still not enough.

Better men than I have struggled to figure out how to live a life of goodness. I try, but I know I'm an utter failure at it. It's a herculean task. I have, sadly, gotten used to soft sheets in the hotels I stay at and, heaven help me, I like good wine. I mean really good wine. And a lot of it. What's more, I have people drive me around because I get road rage even when I am not driving. Yes, you are right: I have become a pussy. Of course, at this point in my life I probably wouldn't give up any of the five-star amenities I now so grudgingly enjoy, but that is why I do benefits and write checks for charity.

Jesus, have you ever heard of anything more impotent than that? I tell you, if I didn't have to live with me, I wouldn't.

I'm also incapable of explaining the inequities in this world. But, truly, can anyone tell me how it is even close to fair that 1 percent of our society has the same amount of money as 90 percent? Seriously. That's not only insane, it's inhuman.

Are we that math illiterate? Is it that difficult to grasp, even at this season when we're supposed to be attentive to goodwill toward others, that something is wrong somewhere in our system if that's what's happening in our world? How many times must we hear it before the inequality of it gets us off our asses and we do something about it? Maybe the other 9 percent who aren't accounted for can help the rest of us out. Jesus Christ!

"Please, Mr. Black," you might say here, "don't take the name of the Son of God in vain."

Really? I'll bet even *he'd* use his name in vain if he wandered around our country and, say, spent a day in Detroit or New Orleans or among the migrant workers or in the urban decay that blights many of our nation's cities. I think Jesus might even utter a couple of good *goddamn*s himself.

"Now you've gone too far, Mr. Black," you might say.

Have I? And how do you know that God doesn't swear? Especially after taking a good look at the human race, it must be a part of his daily ritual.

Okay, enough with the moral arm wrestling. Now I have to get ready for the day ahead.

I have spent most of my last ten Christmases with two close friends of mine and their families and friends. I don't remember where else I have spent Christmas Day, so no doubt I have already pissed off someone I've forgotten because I don't remember shit. Mea fucking culpa. I don't even know when the tradition of my going to visit friends on Christmas Day even started, or why. Probably because otherwise I might not get out of bed and my friends know what will get me up and moving. Food.

Don't get me wrong: it's a real joy to spend time with my friends. I get to drink wonderful wine and enjoy the exceptional meals they prepare. AND I DON'T HAVE TO DO SHIT! You can't beat that.

I don't know why I deserve this. Maybe my friends are really social workers assigned by the state to get me through the loneliness that has overtaken me.

Or maybe they just feel sorry for me.

"Poor Lewis, he really has no one but us. No one should be alone, not on Christmas Day. Not even a Jew with such obvious anger issues that he scares the piss out of children."

So they set up a chair for me and put a place setting

at the dinner table, just like we do for the Prophet Elijah during our seder meal at Passover. Only unlike Elijah, I show up. (As a child, I was always hoping he'd show up, like a Jewish Santa, but he never did. Disappointment runs rampant through all of Judaism, you know.)

But I always show up. They could charge me admission and a two-drink minimum and I'd show up.

Enough with the self-pity, soup's on. I must prepare for the day.

I must shower and shave.

I like the shower, but I love the tub. Is that too personal for you? Sometimes I like to share, and it's not always about being angry. So fuck you. I have something personal to impart.

When I first moved to New York City a bath was the only entertainment I could afford. I'd soak in the tub for hours while reading a book. One of the great joys of my life was reading Stephen King's *The Shining* while marinating myself into prunedom. Even in my thirties, that book scared the shit out of me. Though maybe being naked, and in the tub, and leaving my machete in my other pants had something to do with it, too.

A bath is quiet and calming, not like a shower. A shower is one scalding bitch-slap into reality. When I shower, I try to overcome the depression that arises when I see the few scattered hairs from my head on my hands after I have shampooed and conditioned. Ever so slowly, I have watched my hairline recede and my forehead become more pronounced, like waves pulling away from the beach at low tide, so that soon I will be able to rent the space on my head as signage for hair retrieval products. It's amazing how one can distract oneself from being depressed about one thing by whipping up a good solid depression about something else. Hair loss is much less depressing than feeling alone. Then again, it does remind me that I'm getting old and with that the prospect of marriage and children is fading along with my chances of having hair like my uncle Julie, who when he passed away at seventy-nine had a full head of brown hair and no gray in sight. Genetics, my ass. Many people have said to me that I'm still young enough to have children, and while that may be true biologically, I don't think it makes it right.

As I write this, I'm sixty-one. People say I look great for my age. They are probably being kind. Or maybe they think I'm pregnant. I like to think so. It's nicer than thinking you're fat. I believe I am carrying a Baby Lewie in my belly. Sadly you can't give birth to your inner child. So, first off, I have to find someone I can fall in love with, and vice versa, who can deal with a lifestyle in which I'm home only half the time, and when I'm there she has to deal with unusual habits that have become solidly ingrained through years of living by myself. Like the fact that I spend a part of each day walking around naked. Like I am now, since I got out of the shower. Yes, I walk around naked a lot. Where else can you do that, except in the comfort of your own home?

Unless you're a nudist. I am not a nudist. I don't like being naked outdoors. Too many bugs. And if you brush up against the wrong leaf, you can be scarred for life.

And she's going to have to be someone whom I want to have children with, and she is going to have to be of child-bearing age. That means that she will have to be significantly younger than I am. This leaves one open to all sorts of snide, judgmental asides from family friends and the disapproving public. Even though I tend to ignore being judged, I know that I don't like it. Especially by the people who think everyone should be married and have children so that their existence is validated. Nobody should have to stand and judge me for the actions in my personal life. As long as they're legal, private, and respectful of other people, fuck them. And besides, I've got a whole chorus of voices in my head that sit in judgment of me.

The other problem is that this hypothetical woman is going to have to want to have my child even after she's heard about the drugs I've taken and the, uh, self-indulgent life I've led. That is going to take a real leap of faith on her part for her to believe that my sperm doesn't have seventeen heads, two tails, a Buddha belly, and tiny little hands and still remembers how to swim.

Let us say that this scenario miraculously happens to

work out. By the time I became a daddy—and that's if this all plays itself out very quickly—I would be *at least* sixty-three. The way I see it, that is too old to become a father. No kid needs a father that old. No kid needs to be known as the kid who has the father who should be their grandpapa. No kid needs to spend his time with a parent who is a living lesson in mortality. A child is supposed to watch his dad grow older, not deader.

On the upside—and this is probably only the thinnest layer of silver in a very tarnished and battered lining— my imaginary wife could be lucky enough to have both her husband and her child in diapers at the same time. What's so good about that, you ask? Because she could buy in bulk, and that's a money saver.

Jesus, it was just supposed to be a shower, not some fucking tribunal. On any other day I just hop in the spray, maybe go over what I have to do that day or imagine that a stunningly gorgeous woman is holding the soap . . . but I digress.

My point is that the shower is not the place to be agonizing over life's choices. That's for late nights at a bar, or when something tragic happens and you are forced to face all the crap life can throw at you. Where the specter of death throws a harsh light on all you have done and ever wish to do. A shower is a place for singing, and on Christmas, it's where you should be caroling.

The Carol from Hell

(Based loosely on the "Carol of the Bells")

It's been a year
Let's have a beer
Is one enough?
No, not enough!

I need a shot
Have you got pot?
Where is the scotch?
Please touch my crotch

Ding, dong my schlong
Just dong my schlong

Where is the bong?
I hate this song
Go roll a joint
Oh, what's the point?

Not one good gift
Nothing that fits
Ugly as hell
What is that smell?

Merry, Merry, Merry Christmas
Merry, Merry, Merry Christmas

Oh, stop it now
You stupid cow
Tell Mom to stop
She's serving glop

My head, it aches
What will it take
To make this day
Just go away?

Liquor, Liquor, Faster, Faster
Liquor, Liquor, Faster, Faster

Don't need a hug
Get me a drug
I want to cry
I need to die

Why won't it cease?
Give me some peace
If you're a friend
Just make it end

Ding, Dong, Ding, Dong
This song's too long

WE INTERRUPT THIS BOOK
TO BRING YOU
A MAJOR CATASTROPHE

❄

It doesn't take much to distract me, particularly when I'm doing something that demands concentration, like writing a book and not knowing what the next sentence should be. That does it every time. So instead of my mind going into a laser-like focus in hopes of unraveling the mystery before me and getting on with the next word, it wanders off into every nook and cranny in my increasingly empty head, looking for anything that will keep me from finishing a paragraph in a reasonable amount of time. It will promptly give me a list of all the things I could be doing instead of waiting for the next sentence to reveal itself, because you never know when it will. The arrival of the next sentence is at times much like an erratic and underbudgeted bus service.

And there are things that need to be done. Like, now.

Immediately. They should have been done months ago. How does all this stuff stack up? What am I thinking? Where has my life gone? Why haven't I been a part of it? Why do I keep all these lists of things to do in my head if I am never going to do any of them? Why am I such a lazy shit? How have I managed to waste so much time? Who knows where the time goes? Is it at the back of the closet somewhere—next to the shoes that need to be polished?

God, I have so much to do and there's no fucking time to do it all. Those sweaters that I bought and don't want should have been returned months ago. I still need to return calls and e-mails to over three hundred people. I am behind in contacting a whole town. My piece-of-shit printer needs toner. I really need a new one. And a new computer, too—mine is such a piece of shit that it makes me dream about the joys of using a manual typewriter. And when am I going to find a new cell-phone provider so I have a workable phone instead of just a bad camera that I don't even use? Granted, I need to download those pictures I took two years ago when I was with . . . well, somebody, I don't remember, but they were nice. And I've always wanted to learn another language—French, maybe. When am I going to find the time to do that? It's my life, I should be able to keep up with it, goddamnit. How do people with real jobs and real lives do it? How do they get so much done? And still find the time to go to the gym?

And this is the time when I kick myself for all the many friends I have lost along the way. I am not talking about those who've died but the people I have lost contact with. I haven't stayed in touch. Why? Because I can't get to the next sentence fast enough. See what I mean? Am I making myself clear? Of course not.

So in the midst of my struggle to write something—anything—an epic earthquake hits Haiti. *Haiti!* Are the people there the unluckiest fucks on planet Earth or what? What kind of hideous cosmic joke is this? God certainly does work in mysterious ways, but this time maybe he went too far. Why go after Haitians, who have nothing? To show them that they can have less? Or was God aiming for Miami, got distracted by genocide in the Congo, and he missed? (Wouldn't it have made more sense to go after Las Vegas? Hello! Sodom and Gomorrah. I read the book. There's no mention of poverty-stricken islands anywhere.)

I am not questioning God's wisdom, just his sense of justice. What astonishes me is how many Haitians were in the corpse-ridden streets, singing God's praises. That's a faith that is almost unfathomable to me. I understand it doesn't help under these horrific conditions to bitch, moan, and generally take God's name in vain, but I'm the kind of asshole who gets pissed when the line at the checkout counter is too long. But in the midst of destruction and a tragedy of epic proportions, to be singing God's praises, that's as crazy as my whining.

Am I wrong? Am I missing something? Is it comforting? As I watch the news, I learn that a lot of these people haven't had water in days. Their loved ones are dead. Their houses are rubble. What little livelihoods they had are now gone. The Four Horsemen of the Apocalypse are just around the corner.

"Hallelujah! Praise the Lord! For he hath brought forth the anchor-people, the reporters, the cameramen with video cameras of every size, shape, and description, to cover every square inch of this ever-expanding horror. Hallowed be thy name."

Haiti, don't you see, you are more than just a country now. You are a *story*. A great big goddamn glorious story that will fill the massive flat-screen TVs around the world, where people are leading lives that you can only dream about. Now you've become their dream and they can use it to advertise products that will make their lives oh so much better if they use them regularly, while you sink further into your abyss of misery. Take heart, O Haiti, you are the story, and it doesn't get better than that. Unless we could turn you into a reality show, but no one is ready for reality that's actually fucking reality. Hey, TV viewer, you think your life sucks? Well, give us five minutes and we will show you what the word "sucks" really means. We'll put a smile on your face and sell you a whitener so that those chompers of yours sparkle.

Merry *Christmas*, Haiti. I can't wait for the Christmas Special. *Haiti: After the Tinsel Falls.* Santa visits Haiti to bring toys for everyone, interview survivors, and host special guests Donny and Marie Osmond.

I bet you were wondering how I'd make the catastrophe in Haiti relate to Christmas. See? It was easy. *Everything* relates to Christmas. Everything relates to everything. You can relate any two points in the entire universe. But if you do, be careful: your head might explode.

While I was watching this tragedy unfold, I was struck by the way people around the world reacted, especially here in the United States. Here at home, we actually responded to the catastrophe as if we really were states that were united. There were no arguments about what was the best thing to do. It was just load the trucks and the planes with supplies and food and put the pedal to the metal, we've got some people to save. No one was worried about being a Republican or a Democrat. There was no debating a budget. There were no arguments over which side had the cheapest Band-Aids. There were no words, just action.

There was no fucking discussion, or a discussion of how to proceed with the discussion.

We are quick to help when someone's ass is kicked or when we think someone's ass needs to be kicked. We are great at that. We just don't know how to take care of ourselves. We are a country where many of our people are living on the edge of catastrophe, if not in the middle of it.

Maybe we could turn Christmas into a holiday where we help those who are buried here in our country, only there is no rubble that they lie under or devastation that can be easily shown on CNN. Whether we want to believe it or not, many Americans are living on the *Titanic* in the shadow of the iceberg. Our cities are going down the tubes, our schools are in disrepair, as are our roads and bridges. The once grand city of Detroit is almost leveled and no one seems to give a shit. And New Orleans and its environs are being pounded by shit. More people than I ever imagined are jobless, and many of them have lost their homes. And a lot of people who once were considered middle class now find themselves living on the fringes of poverty.

"Are you trying to turn our beautiful Christmas holiday into a telethon, Lewis?"

No, I just think we should try to help the country out. I mean, just for a few years. Then we can go back to the way it was.

"My kids would kick my ass."

You could get them something. A few gifts.

"They want a lot of gifts, Mr. Black."

What about *better to give than to receive*?

"Nobody buys that shit. Especially kids."

It was just a thought.

"Don't think so much."

It helps pass the time. Merry Christmas.

"Sounds like you want to get rid of Christmas, Mr. Black."

NO. NO. NO. Once and for all, I DO NOT WANT TO DO AWAY WITH CHRISTMAS. I am not the fucking Grinch. I would just like it to be more user friendly. I just think it would be nice if we could share some of our bounty with those less fortunate during this holiday season. Is that so crazy a request? One less gift to the kids, and one that goes out to those among us in need. Then everyone might be lifted up, even if just a little. To some it would be a lot.

Before you grab your pitchforks and torches and chase me through the woods, this was merely a suggestion. Do with it what you will.

Of course I'm not totally delusional. I know what you're thinking.

"Hey, Mr. Black, you've got your own holiday. Go fuck with that, and while you're at it, go fuck yourself."

Fine. Fuck it. What do I know? I'm easily distracted. And you're right. It's not my holiday.

CHRISTMAS DAY, HIGH NOON

If Clothes Make the Man, Then Why Don't We All Dress Like Jesus?

❄

If my Christmas-morning shower is like a tribunal, then finding the right clothes to wear for the day is an out-of-body experience.

For years, I never gave a shit about clothes. They were old, because I was always broke. They were torn, because I didn't know how to sew and had no interest in learning. They were always wrinkled, because I don't like to iron. The upside was no one ever robbed me. And now, lo and behold, all of that is what goes for being fucking fashionable today. When I walk into a store and look at clothes now, it's like I'm looking at all of the shit that was on the floor of my bedroom thirty years ago. Actually, the shit that was on my floor was in better shape than what the best-dressed mannequin is wearing now.

Prewrinkled shirts. What the fuck is that about? Distressed jeans, shoes, and jackets. Are you fucking kidding me? I should have saved my wardrobe in a hamper and set up a boutique men's store. I'd have made a fortune. Why didn't I think of selling worn-out shit and calling it fashion? What's the idea behind it? Is it supposed to make it look like you've been wearing it for years? Are people trying to fake history?

"Yes, I've been wearing these pants since I was fourteen."

And you never grew? You know, I throw out my clothes when they look like that.

Goddamnit, when I wore this kind of stuff, people felt sorry for me or made fun of me. Now it's all the rage, and I am wearing clothes that are ironed and pressed and as neat as they can look on a slouch like me. How is it possible that I am always, always, out of sync with the times? How did I end up living in the crack, which is on the corner between now and then?

I used to just put on whatever was clean—or cleanish—but today is Christmas and my friends are cooking major dinner extravaganzas, so I need to get my act together. I know I can be a prick—yeah, I know myself really well, don't I?—but I would like to honor their day of celebration and all of the hard work they've put into keeping my tummy full by looking like I have spent the time putting together just the right ensemble for such an occasion. (Yes, that's right, ensemble. I can't believe I just used that word in a sentence. What has happened to me?) Dressing myself, which used to be so easy, has now become a painstaking operation. As I've grown older, my wardrobe has increased exponentially, and I can't figure out why or how. It's like the clothes have been mating in the dark closet and when I open the door there are dozens more pieces of clothing in it. It's like a cave full of randy bats or something.

I used to make fun of people who loved their clothes. Now I am addicted to clothing. How do you slowly but imperceptibly become someone you used to make fun of? It's pathetic.

When did clothing become important to me? Is it because I now believe that clothes *do* make the man? What a crock of shit. Clothes don't make anybody. The world overflows with guys who wear really nice clothes and are dicks! You know who they are. They're all around you. At work. At school. The heads that appear on the TV screen and talk to you.

When you see them—and they are every-fucking-where—you realize that a lot of the time, the nicer the clothing, the bigger the asshole.

Maybe what I wear has become more crucial to me these days because I spend a lot of my life in front of people. The more I appeared onstage, the more I became conscious of how I was presenting myself to the public. Even when I had very little money, I started to dress up more for the stage, wearing suits or sport coats with ties. I took this fashion tip from watching idiots utter all sorts of idiotic nonsense, but somehow it was deemed acceptable because they were wearing a tie. I figured if I dressed nicer than the audience, it would calm them down and make it easier for them to handle the shit coming out of my mouth.

"Wow, he's a pig, but he can't be that disgusting, he's wearing a tie—and a very nice one at that," you might think. "He must know what he's doing . . . he can tie a tie."

If I were at a Clothing Anonymous meeting, I would say that my addiction began when I started playing comedy clubs. I was playing a club for five or six days with nothing to do before I had to go onstage. Now, those new employment opportunities gave me the time and the money to go shopping, something I rarely had done till that point. I spent a good chunk of the years I could have spent searching for my soul mate looking for bargains in Macy's or Filene's Basement, back when there was still a real Filene's *basement* in downtown Boston. This may have been where I got hooked on cotton and wool, but maybe that's part of another chapter I could write, "Addictions I Have Known and Walked Around In."

Filene's Basement was a massive space below the Filene's department store. It was a cathedral of inexpensive clothing, and it was where bargain hunters came to worship. There were bins and racks of clothing as far as the eye could see. Each piece came with a price tag with a color-coded dot that would tell you how much it was marked down, anywhere from 40 to 90 percent off, depending on how long the item had been sitting there. The longer it sat there, the cheaper it got. Ninety percent off for a shirt that not only was bright purple and green but with a design on it that, if you moved too quickly, might cause a seizure in an unsuspecting onlooker.

No, you definitely had to search for the true bargain. The twelve-dollar designer dress shirt. Twelve dollars. How do they do it? Who starved to death to make this possible? They must have removed the Crappy label and sewn in a new one. It was the first time in my life that I understood what hunting was like. The joy is in the pursuit, not the kill. (Okay, maybe sometimes the kill, too.) Sometimes in stores I'd pick up something and think, "This is a good buy, but I know there's better somewhere else. Maybe the store down the street. Or in the mall. I know there's better out there, and as God is my witness, I will find it!"

I heard a famous Filene's Basement shopping story a long time ago. Legend has it that in order not to lose their place at a circular rack of dresses, rather than go to a dressing room, women would climb into the middle of the rack and try on their finds. Either you admire the resourcefulness or think that it's crazy. Either way, you'd be right.

Filene's Basement was the place where I discovered nicer clothes than I'd ever worn in my life up to that point. Shirts that didn't feel like cardboard and sweaters that didn't give me the sensation I was dying of extreme eczema. Weird that a discount department store turned me on the same as the first dope dealer I had. I had stopped smoking pot around the time when I was learning to shop, and the last thing I expected was to stumble down the stairs in a Boston department store into a new high. Cotton. Wool. Advanced man-made fibers (which I found didn't really give me the same buzz as natural fibers, but it never hurts to experiment). Though it wasn't long before I was hearing about even better clothing that I could come by for just a few dollars more.

"Really? This is the good shit? Wow!"

"Oh, yes it is, and there's more where that came from, my friend. Hell, yeah, in about six months I'm hooking up with a different supplier and you're not going to even believe how good that shit is, makes this shit look like shit. Now, it's going to be a little more expensive, but you are going to be so glad you won't even care about the cost. You won't believe it. You'll see the difference, you'll feel the difference, and it wears longer. I mean, this isn't just cashmere, my friend. This is baby cashmere. I'm telling you, people kill for these kinds of quality goods."

Who knew there were baby cashmeres wandering around?

I was in a clothing store recently and the salesperson took me to a back room, where the really *fantastic* shit was. You know what I mean: the shit that's so good they keep it a secret unless someone can really appreciate how truly great the shit is. It's just like buying prime dope: you spend a little more for the better shit. And there's always better shit. You don't get addicted so much as you just want to see what the next ounce is like, 'cause it's going to be the really great shit.

So as I look through my closet, it's like a history of highs, with the occasional bummer. A bummer being a piece of clothing that looked stunning on me when the very hot young salesgirl told me it did. Now I stare at a hideous red shirt, as if the shirt had been dyed in blood. She told me it was the kind of thing I should wear.

"Are you sure?" I asked her. "Because I never wear red."

"Red is the new hot color this spring. And I mean *hot*."

"It looks like it's been dyed in blood."

"It's edgy. And edgy is hot."

"Really?"

"It's the kind of thing you probably would never wear—which is why you should wear it. It would surprise people and make you look younger. What are you, seventy?"

What?

"Besides, you know how much women love surprises. Surprises are hot."

Only later, when I put on the shirt at home and looked at myself in the mirror, did I discover that I looked like a diseased radish.

I won't wear a tie on Christmas Day. That's pushing it. But I need something nice, as well as comfortable, because I have two big meals to go to at two different friends' houses, so this is a long day ahead of me. Even though it's not a date and there will be no women I need to impress with my sartorial splendor, I still have to go through all of my clothes carefully. There are shirts that I bought and brought home and have never worn. Exhibit A: the Diseased Radish look; or exhibit B: the Sad Avocado look. (This is why I don't buy clothes for my friends at Christmas. If I don't know what looks good on me, how the fuck would I know what will look good on them?)

"Wait a minute, Lewis," you say. "You go on and on about those in need of food, shelter, and clothing, particularly at this time of year, and you have to hold on to this shirt to prove to yourself that you didn't make a mistake? Are you insane?"

"Well, someday it will catch my eye. And I did write all those checks so I wouldn't feel guilty staring at this overstuffed closet."

"Yeah, but . . ." you might say, then turn away in confusion and disgust.

I don't blame you. I can't explain it either.

Who spends their time having these internal conversations with himself, standing naked in front of an open closet, while knowing full well he is never going to put ON that shirt and wear it? Me, that's who.

But as weird as this is, I also know that this is no day to be experimenting with outfits, no need to look like a deranged peacock on acid, or like a character from *Glee*. So I mix and match and mix and match like I have never seen these clothes before, as if they just magically appeared in my closet. It used to take me a minute to get dressed. Literally sixty seconds. Now it takes me fifteen minutes, easy, to choose my socks. And if I'm getting dressed for a television appearance or some benefit I am hosting, I can go on and on and ON and take up to an hour.

Where did I go wrong? I can seriously melt down over a clothes selection, as I stand there thinking that the fate of the universe depends on my choice of boxer shorts. If I can just find the right color combination and create just the right subtext of panache, my outfit will align with the stars in such a way that I will finally achieve eternal happiness. I will saunter in my silk boxers through a special door in my imagination that takes me back twenty years, but I'll know what I know now and will have the sophistication and maturity to contemplate raising a family. Maybe not *my* family, but somebody's family. I'm kidding, but it does sound kind of appealing, in a sick sort of way.

Damn it, if I'd only worn the right tie I'd be married now and I'd be headed off to one of my kids' houses for Christmas dinner.

It's amazing that one can have these thoughts and somehow avoid being institutionalized.

"Why don't you just wear something red and something green?" one part of me asks.

"You mean radish and avocado," another part of me replies. "I don't think so. No one looks good in radish and avocado."

"Okay, then, put on something that makes you look less fat."

This is easier said than done.

I pull out of my closet something that has line and definition so that I will exude the illusion of fitness rather than the appearance of a pregnant man. It's not a corset, but if they made them for men, someone would make a fortune. I'd even buy one. And I'm not even vain.

So after what feels like I spent most of my afternoon between my closet and my bathroom mirror, I make it out the door.

Finally.

And my Christmas adventure begins.

CHRISTMAS DAY, 1:00 P.M.

Away in a Manger, No Crib for a Bed— Are You Kidding Me?

❄

Since practically every cabdriver in New York seems to have little or no interest in the baby Jesus—yes, I surveyed them; do you think I make this kind of shit up?—the streets on Christmas Day are choked with empty cabs. For God's sake, they should have bid against each other to see who drives me. There's no one on the streets but smiling Hindus, Muslims and Buddhists, Jews, atheists, agnostics, Satanists and Wiccans, free from any form of persecution from the Christian masses, who are huddled around their holiday tree, knocking back the eggnog and listening to Bing Crosby sing "White Christmas."

I grab a cab and head to the Upper West Side, to the apartment of my close friends Willie and Jenny. The Upper West Side has become one of the grand bastions of child-raising on the entire island of Manhattan. People who don't live here believe it's impossible to raise rational, well-adjusted, non-Satanic children in New York City. That somehow this place is a world filled with pederasts, pornographers, exhibitionists, drug addicts, drunks, hookers, and pimps. Bingo! Of course it is. And so is every small town in America. The fact is, they are a very small part of the eight million people who live in the city I call home—some of whom, I admit, are very odd. And while there are all sorts of criminal types here, we also have a lot of policemen—more than 35,000, in fact. So the people who think you can't safely raise a normal kid here don't know what they're talking about. These are the same people who think it's the greatest city on earth, and that it's a nice place to visit, but they wouldn't want to live here. They are crybabies.

Besides, who the fuck determined the ideal place to raise a child anyway? Having a lawn isn't a requirement. It might be nice, I admit—I loved being raised in suburban Maryland—but look at what happened to me. An expanse of well-manicured lawn didn't make me the sane individual who writes this deathless prose that you're reading right now. And a lawn certainly doesn't assure a safe environment. Where better for a poisonous snake to lie in wait for you? And, for God's sake, if we believe the newspaper headlines or the bloviating talking heads on TV, the suburbs are a heavenly green playground for sexual predators.

In my opinion, you can raise children anywhere. ANYWHERE! Don't believe me? Then flip through the pages of a *National Geographic*. Billions—BILLIONS!— of parents raise their children all over the world, in places where there are lions and tigers and bears (oh, my!) and there's nary a lawn chair or Water Weasel in sight. They raise children in boats floating on water. They even raise children in Los Angeles, the only place where you can hear the sound of the void—because there is no fucking "there" there. (Gertrude Stein said that about Oakland. She'd agree with me on this if she were alive today.) So they aren't even raising them in a place, for crying out loud. Children are raised in circuses and in trailer parks. They are even raised in caves. And we in this country have the balls to claim that New York is no place to raise a child. BULLSHIT!

I know that at times parents living in New York must feel like they're raising their kids in an insane asylum, and you find yourself sometimes having to explain things to kids that even you don't understand—"Mommy, why is that man peeing on the sidewalk?" "He's watering it because he thinks it's grass?" or "He's telling the city it needs more public bathrooms." But day to day, life is no weirder here than anywhere else. For God's sake, this whole country is an insane asylum at times.

Trust me, we have no problem raising children. We do have a hell of a time educating them, but that's another book, one that I haven't the time or the patience to write. To put it simply, we want to give our children a great education, but we don't want to pay for it. We adults are the problem. We raise children, we just don't raise them to be adults. I don't know what we are, but most of us sure aren't adults. We never quite make it to fully formed adulthood. We are "childults" or "adulren," if you will.

For example, shouldn't an adult know how to find the place on the wall to hammer in a nail if you want to hang a picture, maybe the Christmas painting your little Tiffany painted of eight Santas pulling a sleigh while Rudolph is in the sleigh, whipping them gleefully. You'd think so, right? Well, I don't. But that hasn't stopped me from destroying many walls in many of the apartments I have lived in. I don't even know what they call that place. It's like the wall's G-spot.

Take a good look at our leadership if you don't believe me. You really think these people are adults? Our leaders don't lead. They spend most of their time running for office, not coming up with good ideas to help us live better lives. They say they have to do it because that's what our election system forces them to do. They say they have no choice. Well, Merry Fucking Christmas, they're wrong. The system works when our elected officials do the job that they were sent to Washington—and to the state capitols and city halls all over the country—to do, which is to lead by example. That means they try to figure out through intelligent compromise and negotiation with the loyal fuck opposition how to solve problems so that each side has a stake in the solution to the problem. The political party that is in power gets a little more say in the wording of whatever the bill or the law is, that's all. It's really pretty simple. It's why we have elections, after all.

What did these idiots we elected do in student government? Spend their time masturbating?

Telling us what you are going to do when you are in power and actually doing it are two different things. And the idiots in office don't seem to understand that anymore. It's like when I think I wrote an e-mail and then I check my e-mail queue and realize I didn't. Just because I had the *thought* doesn't mean I actually did anything about it. These people don't seem to understand that if they actually accomplished stuff while they were in office, the people they represent—that's you and me—might vote for them again. That's the way it used to be.

As a result of running all the time, these douche bags keep their tongues firmly up the asses of whatever corporations or organizations might throw them a buck or two. Hence they can only pay us lip service, because their tongue is somewhere else. And so we get nowhere.

They make things up and call these made-up things "facts" and use them to support whatever bogus idea they are shouting about, and none of them are mature enough to know what our country's best interests are. They know we have "best interests," they just don't have the intellectual curiosity and emotional courage to figure out what they are and then work toward achieving them.

Good fuck luck.

It's Christmas, for God's sake, I've got to get myself back on track here. You can't show up on Christmas spitting venom.

I ask my driver where he is from.

"Kyrgyzstan."

"Wow. I've been there. Well, not exactly there. To our Air Force base. Sadly, I didn't know it was a country till I went there. Sorry."

"No one here does. You a soldier?"

"No."

"You lucky. I was a soldier."

"What brought you here?"

"Freedom. Maybe better life. Two cousins."

"What did you do back home?"

"I was mechanical engineer. Now must learn gooder English for job."

"Better English."

"Yes."

"My dad was a mechanical engineer. I don't know what you guys do, but I know it's important."

"I am Muslim. Not good."

"It's good. It doesn't help, but it's good."

"You see."

"I see."

Great. My cabdriver is a mechanical engineer. You'd think we would need him out there, mechanically engineering whatever needs to be engineered instead of squiring me around town. And I have no doubt that with his knowledge and problem-solving ability we would eventually find the key to achieving energy independence. Oh, well.

What is the matter with us? Jesus, here's this cabdriver who had to get here from Kyrgyzstan—which is a fucking haul, trust me, and might as well be in another solar system—because we were the beacon of freedom shining out there for all to see. We've got freedom, all right, but we still don't know what to make of it. We like to talk about how good it is but in the end it scares us, because we aren't adult enough to handle it. With his newfound freedom, he is now able to drive a cab on Christmas Day, and, with any luck, New Year's, too.

Jesus, I didn't get the kids any gifts again. What is the matter with me?

Hold on a minute. I actually think I have an idea. What if we celebrated Christmas all year round? It's the one time of year people behave with civility. So maybe then our leaders would know how to act, and so would we. Then maybe our kids would, too.

Christmas all year round? That'd make for a *loooong* year for us Jews.

But maybe we'd get more shit done, besides just shopping.

It's something to think about.

CHRISTMAS DAY, 1:15 P.M.

And a Child Shall Lead Them to a Toy Store

❄

Willie and Jenny have two children, and in my eyes they seem to have no trouble raising them in New York City. If you met Gus (who is ten) and Leo (who is seven), you'd have no idea where they were raised. You might even feel that these two were raised in the most charming colonial in the middle of the greenest lawn in the quietest, least violent town in America.

I have no gifts for Gus and Leo. Only once have I ever bought a Christmas gift for the kids. It was a Strat-O-Matic baseball game. (Don't ask.) I got the board game version. (I told you not to ask.) I bought it for Gus, actually. So I've never officially gotten Leo anything. I wonder if he holds a grudge? Do seven-year-old boys hold grudges? Do they relish a seething animosity? I didn't at that age, but then again, at that age I was a saint. Don't believe me? Well, fuck you. I *was*—especially when I compare it to the decades I've spent falling from grace. (It's been a long fall.) The way things are going, I am sure if I weigh the pros and cons I will be going to hell.

Come to think of it, maybe all adults go to hell when they die. That would explain why God would allow an innocent child to die in all sorts of hideous fashions because the only way you get to heaven is when you haven't lived long enough to fuck up in any major serious fashion.

I wonder if maybe Leo is pissed at me. "Wow, here comes Lewis again. What a prick! He never buys me shit for Christmas. He gave Gus that great game once and I got nothing."

Believe me, it's not him. He's a great kid. I just never know what to buy for kids, especially kids who already have stuff that I want, like someone who actually makes food for them, or the newest video game delivery system that delivers state-of-the-state-of-the-art video games.

When Gus and Leo were younger, I didn't want to buy them anything because I was afraid there might be a moving part that would fall off and leap into their mouths, lodging evilly in their windpipes, choking them to death or leaving them twitching uncontrollably because they licked the sealant on some Chinese-made toy, a sealant whose main ingredient is also found in a secret nerve gas they were working on for the military.

I hate to sound like one of those people, but from time to time I become one of those people. But in my more lucid moments—and I know they aren't that often—I wonder: How come no child where I was brought up ever choked to death on a toy? Were kids choking and the adults just hiding the fact from us? Did they have a special burial place for them? Seriously, what were we doing differently then, in a time when people didn't hesitate to drive drunk, women smoked while pregnant, and seat belts were summarily ignored in every car that had them? How is it we are paying more attention now and getting fewer results? Is it because society sobered up? Do drunks, because they are drunk, pay more attention to what's in front of them?

These are questions that keep me up at night. Seriously.

And then I wonder: What the fuck has happened to us? Are toys worse for us now because we don't make toys in this country anymore? Sure, we had polio and tuberculosis to contend with, but our toy chests were never threats to our health and well-being. (Call me crazy, but never once did I say, "That toy looks delicious, I think I'll shove it down my throat.")

Leo may be holding a grudge because I never gave

him a gift when all I was really trying to do was keep him out of harm's way.

What do I say to him if he meets me at the door, waiting for me to give him a present? "I didn't get you anything for Christmas, Leo, because on the advice of my attorney I do not want to be held liable for your death"? I don't need that kind of pressure during the holidays. Merry Christmas, indeed.

So I arrive, with nothing for the children. But I have made purchases for some of the adults. I know how to shop for them. They won't choke on my gifts. Even the bottle of wine I will give to Willie's brother, Rob, will be drunk responsibly. And even if he drinks the whole bottle by himself, the worst that will happen is he'll write a very sad melody, weep uncontrollably for hours, and fall asleep in a heap on the floor. When he wakes up, his eyes will be a little puffy and his head may ache but, goddamnit, he will be alive.

There's still time. I could stop and pick up something for the kids. Ah, fuck it, whatever I buy them will just be a disappointment. At least this way I am consistent. Consistency is better than a fruit basket. Or disappointment. Besides, they've got the great video game. I don't.

Hell, let 'em choke on their resentment of me.

MEDITATIONS OF A
JEWISH SANTA

I have always felt somewhat isolated at Christmastime, so it would never have crossed my mind to play Santa Claus. Ever. It's not even a part that I was eager to play when it was offered to me. I mean, it would be a stretch for me, a big stretch—but you don't grow as an actor playing Santa. It doesn't lead to other roles.

"Did you see Lewis Black's Santa? It was the definitive Santa. Breathtaking. I'd love to see him play other really fat jolly men. Who thought he had it in him?"

I certainly didn't. Maybe it's because I was raised Jewish, though not severely Jewish. We were the "No, we are *not* bringing a Christmas tree, Chanukah bush, or any other tree into this house" kind of Jewish. I don't ever remember even asking my parents if we could have a tree. But even if I did, the answer would have been no.

Those were the rules. (And that was about as Jewish as we got.)

Even as I've grown older and shared in the Christmases of my friends or my girlfriends' families, I have never felt a part of the multitude of joys that seem to infuse the Christmas season. People can call it "the holiday season" all they want, but the feeling of "Christmas" has always passed me by—like the last empty cab in the middle of a thunderstorm.

"One really shouldn't say 'Merry Christmas,'" these idiots say. "To be truly politically and socially correct, one should say, 'Happy Holidays.'"

Really? We're awash in a series of problems that make this the most crippling decade I've lived through. We're pounded with so much information every second of our lives that we have forgotten what the facts are. We've spent ten years bleeding ourselves dry as we fought extraneous wars that had nothing to do with reality, let our nation's infrastructure and educational systems rot and crumble, bloated our health care system until it's beyond repair and our economy has barely survived greed of epic proportions. So in the midst of all of this, we feel the urge to argue over the use of the word "Christmas" at Christmastime? ARE WE TOTALLY FUCK INSANE?

Does anybody honestly think that somehow this debate will change the world? Or make it a better place?

Let me make it easy on you: IT'S CHRISTMAS-

TIME! You have the inalienable right as granted by our Constitution to Happy whatever you want. It makes no difference to life on this planet or the indifferent universe we find ourselves stumbling through if you spout "Merry Christmas" rather than "Happy Holidays." You can say "Happy Horseshit" if you want to, if you're not within earshot of children or adult crybabies.

As you can see, I don't even have the time or the energy to muster a rational argument against such inexcusable bullshit.

Think about it another way: By putting the mute button on a simple "Merry Christmas," you destroy the sense of separation that gives me such joy. For one brief moment, in the expression of just two words, I am made unique by nothing I had done, just by being born.

It could be the reason I have no real feeling for Christmas is the claustrophobic and cloying warmth of it all. The soundtrack at this time of year clogs one's ears with an overly sweet syrup of songs about homes too happy for my taste and hearths too inviting to be believed. I am surrounded by too many people who are just a little too happy to see each other, even though they have never seen each other before in their lives. All of a sudden, after making it through another dismal year of none of this type of "what a joy it is to be alive" behavior, it's all way too hard for me to believe it's real. (Or to stomach.)

It's all beyond my comprehension. Or it could be I'm

just a jaded prick who doesn't believe in the magic this season possesses.

Yeah. That sounds about right.

I have never thought much of Santa Claus. Jewish parents make absolutely sure that their children will never believe in him during their formative years. If Jewish children did, imagine the madness that would ensue. We could bring down Judaism just by demanding that our parents recognize the reality of Santa Claus. But that will never happen, as Jewish parents destroy the whole idea of a gift-giving saint with the simplicity of pure logic.

"Really, how come there's a different little Santa at every mall and store we go to, huh?" they say.

Or: "If there's a Santa, then there's only one Santa. There shall be no other Santas before you except the one true Santa. But he doesn't exist, because he isn't there."

This one's nice, too: "If you really think there's a Santa, why don't you sit on the front steps all night in the freezing cold and see if he climbs down any chimneys tonight. Good luck. And since we're a family that isn't lucky enough to have a chimney, how would Santa get into our house? Does he bring a locksmith with him? And it would probably have to be a Jewish locksmith, because a Christian locksmith is going to want to be home with his family. And how many Jewish locksmiths are there? None."

Whoo.

As a result, by the time I was five, I knew that Santa was just some impotent cartoon figure. Or a slob in a red suit with bad breath who hung out at the mall.

As my parents tormented me, I tormented my Christian friends by harassing them for their ignorant, blind belief in a nonexistent Kris Kringle. It was fun bursting their bubble. If my parents were going to take away a bit of the innocence of my youth, well then, I was going to do the same to my friends.

So it was more than strange that four decades later I found myself on a film set, stuffing myself into a fat suit, then putting on the red suit, the beard, and getting ready to play Santa Claus in the movie *Unaccompanied Minors*. There is something daunting about donning the outfit of Old Saint Nick and all that it entails. There is also something completely idiotic about it. Well, except for the shiny boots. I admit, I kind of dug the boots.

Yet there I was, the red-faced man of anger—an anger verging perpetually on a stroke—transformed suddenly into the red-faced man of jolliness and mirth. The irony was inescapable.

There is a certain release one experiences when one is given the opportunity to actually expel a few *Ho-ho-ho*s into the air as Santa Claus, and thanks to the whole getup, one doesn't look like an asshole. (However, you just can't stand on the street bellowing "Ho-ho-ho" without some real trouble heading your way. Trust me on this one.) It's not as liberating as letting a few *Fuck*s fly, but it will do in a pinch, if you're willing to look like an idiot.

There's also something nice about taking off a fat suit and feeling like you've lost weight, so that your own fat doesn't seem so fatty anymore. It's a thinner fat. For a moment I felt lean and mean again, even young, but that good feeling passed as soon as I put on my own pants again.

Still, when I was in costume, the cast and the extras had to act like this was all very real and that I was Santa Claus himself. The scene didn't even call for me to contend with kids sitting on my lap. Thank God. I wasn't sure I could really handle that end of the Santa package.

Then I had to.

Fast-forward several years. Once again I found myself putting on the fake fat for a holiday special I hosted for the History Channel called *Surviving the Holidays with Lewis Black*. I was to play an actual Santa at a New York store. Now there were real kids—wide-eyed, sad-eyed, cross-eyed, snot-ridden, full of wonder, full of fear, full of life. Real live kids.

Sitting there in Santa's chair, all dressed up like Old Saint Nick himself, you look down into the eyes of these kids, who are staring at you as if you really are who you're pretending to be. You start to realize that there's something eerie about the whole experience, being awash in all of that innocence, that hope. Especially when you're the one who has never bought into any of this happy claptrap. It was a real test of my acting ability, and I didn't think I was up to it. After all, I'm not Mr. Warm and Fuzzy. I find it exhausting. And you can't fool kids.

It's bizarre at best to be a middle-aged Jew dressed up as Santa Claus whose job it is to ask a kid what he wants for Christmas, knowing full well you can't deliver the goods. I pretty much felt like the head of FEMA during the Katrina crisis. So here I was, potentially setting these youngsters up for a bitter disappointment. As their little feet scuttle down the stairs on Christmas morn, only to find that the kitten, the favorite doll of the year, the year's greatest new toy, or the miniature pony that they asked for and you said would be delivered isn't there.

You created expectations that wouldn't be fulfilled, and were never going to be by the likes of you. You might as well have taken a shit under the tree for all the goodwill you created.

You destroyed their Christmas.

Or maybe you should look at it in a more positive light. Maybe, you conclude, you've prepared those children for what truly lies ahead for them: disappointment and despair. Learning that at an early age will leave them better prepared for real life than that happy kid who got the new virtual-reality hoohah that everyone wants but is so tough to find. But he got it. That hardly ever happens. Stores run out of it. Just like doctors will someday when they hand out, say, the cancer vaccine. By the time they get to you, "Sorry, we ran out." Bastards.

After playing Santa twice, I can't figure out who enjoys being Santa. In the end, you're just a big, fat, compulsive liar. You're no savior; you're just leading a child to his first disappointment, the first of many. Soon the child's eyes are opened and he's screaming at his parents: "Santa's not real? Are you shitting me? Who ate the cookies and milk all those years? You, Dad? Why, you son of a bitch!"

Though I've never experienced this happy moment of revelation, even I know it's got to be tougher than losing one's virginity. This is the moment when the trust and the faith that you had in your parents—your guardians and protectors—can't be relied on anymore. What else have they been lying to me about? Are they even my parents? Maybe I'll fall asleep one night and wake up the next morning in a ditch by the side of the road. There'll be a note from them that says: "Don't worry. Santa will come pick you up in a minute, unless you were sleeping when he arrived to get you. Santa doesn't like that. He'll just be on his merry way. So, good-bye. Good luck. Oh, by the way, we aren't real, either." Guess I won't be sleeping anymore.

. . .

So on the set, I sat there and ho-ho-hoed as I lifted each one of those kids onto my knee. They looked into my eyes with a mixture of bewilderment, joy, and a deep-seated mistrust. Some of them just seemed to be in panic mode, and some of them knew it was all bullshit. Yet they were ready to expound on all of their wishes, from the most materialistic to wanting there to be world peace.

I sat through all of it. Gasping for air through a beard that I swear was made from recycled fiberglass. And the costume I wore had apparently been dipped in some sort of heavy-duty industrial sealant. (It had all the breath-ability of a rubber suit.) My pores were weeping as I stewed in my own juices, sweating like a porker.

After a while your brain can't stop screaming, "It's fucking hot as hell" as you gaze down at the child in your lap and try to utter with some semblance of a smile on your face, "And what would you like Santa to bring you for Christmas?"

"Rmph cahhblooe sna pootay."

"What did you say? I didn't hear you, my dear little angel." I didn't hear you because all I can hear are the screams from my overheated scalp. Or maybe they're coming from that area that lies between my brain and my skull. Maybe it's just because as much as I want to, I don't really give a shit.

"Anda yelpx dafutti conna socala puche froome and hahahaha tee tee."

"Oh yes, I will get you the dafutti and everything else you asked for," I reply, praying that I'm close to understanding what the kid asked for.

"What's a dafutti?"

"I don't know, you asked for it. And you're going to get it." Sweat pours down my brow like water over Niagara Falls. I feel like I'm running a marathon while basting in my own perspiration.

The whole thing isn't right. I am dying. Right now, dressed in a fat suit and fake beard, I'm dying. No one sweats like this and lives. Please get this kid off my lap before I am forced to tear these clothes off so I don't die of heatstroke.

Who the hell does this to themselves more than once? What sadistic world do we live in that allows such abuse to occur?

A raging alcoholic is who. Someone who throws back six tumblers of chablis before going to work, and brings with him a flask filled with crème de menthe just to get through the day. It's the only way you could possibly stand this. I drink, therefore I am Santa.

I know, you're not supposed to drink around kids. Which is why I didn't. But to do this more than once demands more mind-altering substances than I have access to.

After playing Santa, I now think that at the end of that wonderful old movie *Miracle on 34th Street*, when Maureen O'Hara and John Payne realize that the nice old man played by Edmund Gwenn is actually Santa, they should do the human thing:

Electrocute him.

CHRISTMAS DAY, 1:45 P.M.

Here Comes the Old Giftless Jew!

❄

Thank God my friends don't ask me to dress up as Santa. I'd have to kill them.

"Here we are," the driver informs me as we pull up.

As I enter the home of Willie and Jenny, I encounter the first Christmas tradition: the disappointed gazes of Gus and Leo.

"Oh, it's you, Lewis," they say, sounding let down. I know what they are thinking. "We believe in Santa. We know he doesn't exist, but we still believe in him. We just don't believe in you, Lewis. No gift? Really? Again?"

Then they hightail it to the back rooms of the apartment. No doubt to hide their disgust at the stinginess of their dad's stupid, cheap friend.

Wait a minute, why am I letting them upset me and undermine my festive fuck demeanor? *They* didn't buy *me* anything, did they? They didn't make an effort either. Yes, I feel better now.

The living room is filled with members of Willie's and Jenny's families. (And, of course, a Christmas tree, which towers over me, even though I am taller than it. Figure *that* out, genius.) They are hovering over the hors d'oeuvres. There is, however, always something a bit existential about the gathering. ("Existential"—now there's a word you rarely use anymore, unless you're in college and are wandering the campus, feeling ennui because you just read Camus's *The Stranger* and didn't understand it. In fact, "ennui" is another one of those rarely used words that only comes to mind when one thinks about existentialism. It really is a vicious cycle.) It's not the folks themselves who make it feel strange in that existential way. A few faces may change from year to year, but the people Willie and Jenny invite are all folks I enjoy spending time with. Not an asshole in the bunch. And everybody knows that, come the holidays, assholes make things unbearable, not existential. They're the human version of the turd in the punchbowl. And I think they all feel the same way about me. They are all warm and welcoming. Or else they're all just too polite to let on otherwise.

I can't put my finger on it, but as I stand there, I think that maybe things used to be more Christmassy in the good old days, back when women wore hoopskirts and people uttered words like "poppycock." Not like today, where it's entirely possible that the men are wearing the hoopskirts and the "poppycock" is some kind of Internet porn sensation, or the name of a gay snack food. Information traveled so slowly in those days that it must have been a world of continual discovery. It must have seemed like a miracle to see people you know all gathered in one place. And if one could believe in Jesus, surely one could believe in Santa. It was a time when one wore so many clothes, and had to make sure that the horse and carriage were taken care of when you went to Aunt Pittypat's for Christmas dinner. The snow was snowier then because there were fewer chemicals in it. So by the time one finally got settled around the hearth and raised a glass in toast, one truly felt thankful to have gotten there at all.

"My stars, Jeremiah! The womenfolk were certain the trip was too arduous and insisted you wouldn't make it for the festivities. But I said balderdash to that kind of talk. Balderdash I say again—and Merry Christmas to one and all."

Nowadays, Christmas seems to be a backdrop, in front of which we band of merry old souls gather. We are not so immersed in the holiday spirit as we would have been in times past. In fact, we're separated from it. We can point at it and comment on it, but not really wrap ourselves up in it the way our grandparents could.

No, I am not stoned.

"Maybe the folks in the apartment a few floors above

us are more immersed in holiday cheer," I think. "They could be using up all the Christmas in the building. Maybe they are so desperate to enjoy themselves, they took more than their fair share of the holiday. Maybe Christmas is like oxygen in a confined space, and there is only so much to go around."

No, that's insane. Maybe I *should* be stoned.

"Well, for God's sakes, Mr. Black, of course there's an existential feel in the festive holiday air that we Christians share, for you, my friend, are a Jewww."

That's not the reason. I know it isn't.

"Maybe you have arrived on the scene after the joy of Noël had come and gone," you say.

No. They don't open their gifts until after we have our Christmas dinner. That's when I know it's time to leave. I don't need to sit through the icy stares of Gus and Leo and whatever other children are there whom I haven't gotten a gift for.

"Existential? How? In what way? Maybe next Christmas you should give Gus and Leo copies of Sartre and Camus, Uncle Stranger."

It's about this time that I wonder if maybe I just have the flu.

And then there are my good friends Willie and Jenny, the ones who gather this tribe together.

Jenny was raised in New York, too, and by a couple of geniuses, no less. Willie was raised by wolves. (I'm kidding. It would be fun, though, to be raised by wolves—until the authorities came and grabbed you and shot your parents, of course. That would suck. Willie was actually raised in New Jersey, which is, contrary to popular belief, very nice. But I'd still rather be raised by wolves.)

I have known Willie for thirty years. He is the head writer of the *New Electric Company* and has spent years composing musicals with his brother, Rob. He is also the founder of The 52nd Street Project, a mentoring program for the kids in that neighborhood. For that he was given one of those MacArthur "genius" grants. Trust me, he is no genius. Ingenious, but not a genius.

Willie is married to Jenny, who is a lovely woman with brainpower to spare. Now, if she were the reason they said Will was a genius, I would concur. I would concur wholeheartedly. To be absolutely fair, however, that he was able to hide his myriad faults long enough to trick her into marriage just might be proof of his genius.

Jenny was the associate producer for nine years at the Williamstown Theatre Festival in Massachusetts and has since moved on to be a producer at the Public Theater in New York City. She was one of the main producers behind the hugely successful Broadway revival of *Hair*. And as I type, she has just become the first woman to be named the artistic director of the Williamstown Theatre Festival.

The reason I have given you my friends' résumés is to help you understand how extraordinary it is to me that two people in the same business—show business, no less—could have not only very successful careers, but also a very successful marriage and raise two lovely children. They not only have done this but they are generous enough to expand their family circle to include somebody like me.

As many people who do it know, it's tough when both members of a couple are pursuing full-time careers. You have your shit, and they have their shit, and now you have all the shit that a marriage can bring to the table. It's a lot of shit, and if you have kids, then you've added their shit on top of your shit. You have to keep reminding yourself that the kids' shit is just as important as yours, and then you have to remind yourself that your shit is as important as theirs. I imagine it's like living in the emotional equivalent of an Escher drawing.

And he's a Catholic and she's a Jew. That can open a whole other can of worms, but it hasn't for them.

Yet, in spite of all of this, Willie and Jenny have a "traditional" marriage.

I have enough trouble just dealing with myself and my career without being half insane most of the time. How the fuck do people do it? How the fuck do they make such a deep commitment to each other without going completely batshit?

I stand in awe of them. Well, maybe not in awe. I'll

save that for something truly beyond the realm of my belief system. But . . . this is close to that.

And every Christmas Day I have spent with them, I envy the life they have fashioned together. And wonder what the fuck is wrong with me.

CHRISTMAS DAY, 2:00 P.M.

6,500 Calories, Not Counting the Three Bottles of Wine

❄

I spend the first hour after my arrival catching up with everyone. Since I spend most of my life traveling from city to city, performing, it's nice to hear about the accomplishments and the bullshit and the nonsense. It's soothing to know that life—real, normal human life—goes on. That over the last year the kids have been doing well and have gone on to the next grade and that school is good. That someone—not me—got a raise. That someone else—again, not me—has found a better job. It's nice to notice that the marriages seem to get stronger with the years. Maybe it's just a front they put up for the holidays, and deep down they are all eating their insides out. That after the party, they go home and return to their lives of shared bitterness, oppressive claustrophobia and boredom. They all go to bed that

night thinking about how wonderful it must be to be me.
"Oh, if I were only Lewis. Single. Fancy free. Devastat-
ingly handsome. No one to answer to. He must be living
a wonderful life."

What a life, huh?

Somehow I doubt anybody thinks any of that. I can
see that my friends are happy with their lives, their children, and what they are building together. It's always
very comfortable as I sink into a very cushy chair and
toast their accomplishments with a very nice glass of
red wine.

At this moment, as I sip my wine and am surrounded
by friends, I always think of my brother, Ron. He has
long since left the planet, but I still miss him terribly,
especially at times like this. He is the one who truly introduced me to the splendors of red wine when he was
living in France. I visited him there—yes, when I was
broke and he had to pay for my plane ticket—and we
spent some time in the vineyards and over numerous
glasses of the grape. He was passionate about wine and
food years before the concept hit our shores. He would
have loved this moment when the glasses were being
filled. He and Willie would have taken this moment and
turned it into a half-hour discussion about the friskiness
of the grape.

If wine weren't enough for male bonding, when Ronnie and Willie got together to cook, it was scary. They
could carry on for days about how to really cook a lamb.

Right. Like the lamb cared. As they would debate all of the permutations of preparation, spices, and cooking time, they would twitch with glee. They were like crackheads getting ready for their next fix. Sometimes it really freaked me out. Okay, not *sometimes*. Always. It always freaked me the fuck out.

It upsets me that my brother never got to see America's changed attitude toward food. He was blogging about restaurants when he lived in France before there even was "blahginnnnng." This was in the late eighties, when hardly anyone in America gave a shit about food. This was before supersizing your fast-food meal was all the rage and cardiologists from one end of this country to the other were building additions to their houses. For God's sake, he missed the arrival of the Food Network. Talk about life not being fair. Or maybe it is. Maybe he would have lost his mind watching it. So many kitchens, so many cuisines, and so little time. Goddamnit. This was his era, "the golden age of food."

I am always saddened when I think about all of the things we never had the chance to share. (If there's a true downside to Christmas, it's remembering all of the folks who have passed on along the way, all that you have lost. Christmas may be about the birth of the baby Jesus, but it also makes you think a lot about the people you want to spend time with but can't anymore.)

Yum. This wine sure is tasty. Remember, Lewis, you have to pace yourself. You're starting your Christmas celebrating at 1:00 p.m., and you won't be done until at least midnight, so don't go overboard too early. Take small sips, Lewis, very small sips. I've never been good at drinking during the day. This is a marathon, and there's no way to train for it, and if you did, you'd have to go to rehab by the time New Year's Eve rolled around.

I also have to keep an eye on my food consumption. I am facing two huge meals that day, from a dazzling array of appetizers to a scrumptious series of desserts. And I love food. Not in a foodie way, in a love way—a deep, abiding adoration and worship kind of a way. I live and breathe to be immersed in a universe of tastes.

I'm not an idiot. I know two massive meals in a day is wrong. It's bad for my health. Bad for my stomach, bad for my large intestine. Bad for my small intestine. Bad for my colon (which I think is either my large or small intestine, I can't remember). It's bad all around. And it's greedy and piggish and self-indulgent.

Let's face it, there's no excuse for this kind of behavior. People all over the world are starving and on this day I eat what a family of eight might consume in a week. But, God help me, that doesn't stop me.

I am like a locust on Christmas Day, and as I chew through everything that's set in front of me, from olives to exotic cheeses to dried meats to chips and dips to clams casino to the hindquarters or forequarters or whatever quarters of the cow I find before me, one thought haunts me.

"Did I write a big enough check to America's Harvest to make up for this gluttony?"

I never know. One of the great things about me—and that category is a narrow one—is I don't need people around me to be judgmental about my behavior. Nobody is more judgmental about me than me. It's a gift.

So I wonder will God show me pictures of this day when he consigns me to the third ring of hell, where one is forced to view videos of buffets from around the world for an eternity and beyond?

But if I don't come to Christmas dinners with my friends, what am I supposed to say to them?

"Well, no, I can't make it this year because I'm afraid I will face eternal damnation for eating one too many chèvres. . . . Oh, you're only serving two. Never mind. I'll be there."

As I ponder my sin, while sipping my second glass of wine, Willie and Jenny are preparing another incomparable meal. How the fuck do these people do it?! They have jobs, two children, friends, God knows what other concerns, and they cook great food! Where do they find the energy? How can they be so happy as they sweat over all of these ingredients? How do they know it's not going to taste like shit?

I don't remember the last time I cooked. I used to cook, a looooong time ago, when I had no money and no choice. I was a lousy cook—big surprise, I know—

but I cooked. Nothing very fancy. I mean, I could toss a salad (and no, not like in prison, for a guy named Sheet Rock, but with fresh greens), and I did, for a time, bake my own bread. No one believes I did; even the people who watched me do it think I am lying. But I did. Wheat bread, mostly. No baguettes or anything else that might require a little thought or energy—just run-of-the-mill wheat bread. It was tasty, but it was never a full-blown loaf. I never got it to fully rise. Every loaf I made was always somewhere between matzoh and Pepperidge Farm. Still, it was bread. You could cut it with a knife and put a pat of butter on it. It worked like the butter delivery system it was meant to be. It used to give me a great deal of satisfaction.

What's happened to the world? When I made bread, I knew it was shit, but at least other bread was good for you. Now people say that bread isn't good for you. When did the geniuses of the world decide that? Where did they hold that meeting? It's bread, for fuck's sake, it's the staff of life. Where are the Bible beaters now? How come they aren't defending bread's right to be eaten? Now if you want to eat a sandwich, you need to jog, absercize, or elliptiodalize. Oh, spiteful bread with all your stinking carbs, where did you go wrong? What happened to the Harry the Homemaker who used to dwell within me? Did all the carbs kill him?

Willie and Jenny take such joy in preparing the meal.

And for my part, I take great joy in eating it. Cooking, I just don't have the time for it anymore, but boy, do I have time to eat the whole day away.

At the table, the conversation focuses on the food. The table begins to hum with the satisfaction that comes from a fine meal. The room is filled with the purring sounds of satisfied eaters.

"Really, it's not that difficult. All you do is take out the bone marrow and slowly cook in a port reduction and then let the short ribs marinate in that for a week."

"Where do you two get the fucking time to do this?" I almost shout at them. But then I remember that there are tender ears at the table as well as my own, so I merely wonder to myself. All I know is, I would have an easier time putting the short ribs back in the cow than I would preparing the dish that sits before me.

Jenny's sister, Jilian, prepares the dessert. It is, as usual, stupefying. It's always a sensational sugar delivery system. Sometimes it even includes sugar spun into a work of art. I weep. She has an infant, and she's a master pastry chef with a full-time job. Isn't there an Olympics for people like her? People who can do all sorts of things really well and spin sugar at the same time? It makes a lot more sense than those folks who cross-country ski and then stop and use the rifle they're carrying to shoot at targets. What the fuck is that supposed to be about other than some kind of sick World War II Scandinavian flashback?

This time we are having tiramisu, and there is a bonus dessert, which I have forgotten, because of the obvious sugar shock I went through. But it was worth it. If I were told I had to get diabetes for a major movie role, I would have Jilian prepare my dessert every night.

After dinner and coffee and some more terrific conversation, it's time for me to go. I rise slowly from the table. One last time I toast my hosts and all who have gathered together.

I am overwhelmed by this sense of family that I am allowed to glimpse and share in. It has taken a bit of the sting out of the loneliness I always feel on this day. Yet it makes me yearn for what I know I shall never have. A family of my own. Thank God there's another meal ahead to distract me from these thoughts.

It's time to take my bloated frame downstairs and catch a cab from the Upper West Side of Manhattan to the Upper East Side. I move slowly. Very slowly. It's time for the next round of appetizers. And only one thought consumes me as I climb into the taxi heading for my next destination: If there really is a Saint Nick, they will be serving pigs in a blanket. Granted, it's not an elegant offering, but they are delightfully simple and delish.

CHRISTMAS DAY, 5:30 P.M.

If It's Really over the River
and Through the Woods,
I'm Not Going to Make It

❄

In the cab on the way to my friend Neil's apartment, once again I am alone. As I sit in the backseat in silence—New York City is pretty quiet on Christmas afternoon as we drive through Central Park—I have some time to think. That's what I need, more time to think.

And boy, do I think.

I wonder why it is that the overwhelming drive that brings couples together to procreate somehow completely missed my gene pool. My brother and his wife never wanted to have children, either.

Salmon swim upstream to do it.

Penguins go through hell to do it.

Rams crack their skulls to do it.

At what point along the way did my DNA say, "Ah, fuck it!"? It wasn't just my upbringing or a bad marriage. It has to be deep in the genetic blueprint of one's being, like wherever it is that diseases come from.

Is it a mutation? Was there someone in my family tree who masturbated so much that the sperm forgot their purpose for being there in the first place?

Was a meal served to one of my ancestors that was so intoxicating that it created a genetic obsession with food that replaced the drive in me that ensures the survival of the species?

Did some woman chomp down hard on my great-great-great-grandfather's nuts?

Whatever it was, it couldn't have been good.

Maybe my brain believes that since I look pregnant and feel like I am carrying a Baby Lewie down there, that I don't need to procreate.

As I come to these unsettling—and un-Christmassy—conclusions, I knead my stomach like dough, in order to move Baby Lewie over to make room for more food.

The Upper East Side of the city, where Neil lives, is a part of town that's a little more hoity and a bit toitier than the Upper West Side. Neil is neither. He is the kind of person who will surprise you. He doesn't even look like an Upper East Sider, which in my mind is a combination of Donald Trump and Joan Rivers. For one thing, his hair is long—really, really long. It goes all the way down his back. He looks like he should be playing bass in a rock band. Not surprisingly, Neil has one foot firmly jammed in the heart of the sixties. On the Upper East

Side, most people's feet are jammed in the heart of the fifties—the 1850s, when servants did everything but wipe your ass for you (and maybe even did that). It's the type of neighborhood where one feels entitled to feel entitled.

Neil is the antithesis of that. He works way too hard to ever assume that kind of attitude. He doesn't tolerate that kind of attitude, yet he loves the neighborhood where the entitled flourish. He still says things like: "You're either on the bus or off the bus." Neil says it with real authority, like he is absolutely certain of its import and its meaning. Sometimes when he says it, it scares people.

More importantly, the reason he's not a real Upper East Sider: HE WAS ACTUALLY AT WOODSTOCK!

He really was. Honest. I am not kidding. He even remembers some stuff that happened there. Sometimes I make him tell me about it, and then I forget that he told me, so it makes me feel like I was there.

Sadly, there will come a time very soon when there'll be a television interview with the last person alive who was actually at Woodstock. I really hope it's Neil.

The two of us met at the Yale School of Trauma—I mean Drama. He was in the technical program. I was never sure what these guys did there, but it was very technical. Neil now owns and runs Hudson Scenic Studio, the largest scene shop in New York. He has built the sets of an impressive number of shows from off-off-Broadway to Broadway. The body of his work has garnered him a Tony Award. The son of a bitch knows what he's doing.

While he's accomplishing all of these amazing feats of stagecraft, he also found the time, energy, and stamina to be married three times. Physicists haven't come up with a formula for that kind of energy. He really seems to like being married. He married young, and like many of those young marriages of our era, it ended nineteen years later in divorce court. His second wife, Laurie Beechman, was an extraordinary theatrical performer and exceptional singer. She died of ovarian cancer. They fell in love when she was in remission, and after they were married the cancer returned. Love doesn't conquer all, but that's because life is brutally unfair.

If it were me, I probably wouldn't have gotten married again. But while life may be unfair, it also has its beautiful moments, and so Neil met Machiko, who is now his wife. She worked for a company that did all of Michael Bloomberg's financials, taxes, and God knows what else. Yes, that Michael Bloomberg, New York City's billionaire mayor who has more money than God. She was a financial analyst. I don't know what they do but when they do it right, somebody makes a lot of money, and if they are wrong, somebody gets fucked. She is razor sharp and has a keen mind and, with all of that, even a lovely smile. How my friends manage to fool these beautiful, intelligent women into marrying them is a mystery for the ages.

Machiko spends her time taking care of their daughter and works on a variety of fund-raising projects and figures out where we are all going to go for Thanksgiving. They are very happy. She has made Neil slow down, which means he still uses more energy than any three people I know.

The story of their marriage is unusual, which is putting it mildly. Before Neil and Machiko met, Neil had what can only be described as a one-night stand with a beautiful young woman, the result of which is she got pregnant. (Please, hold whatever recriminations you have to yourselves.)

In light of all the couples I have known over the years who've taken years to conceive and have turned to fertility specialists, here is my pal Neil, who falls into bed with a woman he barely knows and in one shot he does it. I can only call it astonishing. (I'd love to know what the statistics are on pregnancies after a one-night stand, but as this is a Christmas book and we're veering into some unusual territory here, let's move on. Then again, Christmas is all about a certain baby. . . . Nah, better not.)

You can certainly ask what were these two people thinking, but you could also ask: What was God thinking? Surely he knows better than that.

It turns out, he does.

And then, Bingo! Neil's a dad.

The woman wanted to be a mother. And even though Neil is Catholic and wasn't looking to get married or to live with the mother, he was thrilled about becoming a father. So he and the child's mother came to a legal arrangement and several months later, a beautiful baby girl was born——hang on to your hats, and your sense of irony——on Christmas Day.

I realize that for the traditional family-values folks, this is way too far-fetched a way to make a family. There are numerous Americans that hold on to the concept of the traditional marriage like a dog and its favorite bone. It makes them feel better to believe that a family unit is a mother and a father and their children and that's that and that's the way God planned it. For years this concept kept alive millions of loveless marriages and no doubt created sexual arrangements that ranged from the Neanderthal to the Gothic, in their wake creating family environments that were nastily toxic, not only to the parents but to their offspring as well.

I don't know at what point the traditionalists will finally get it, but a family now comes in many, many forms, and as long as there is a loving environment, then one could be raised by wolves——gay wolves, for Christ's sake. If I learned anything from having a child that wasn't mine, it's that every child is yours and should be treated as such, unless of course they happen to be a snotty little prick. Isn't that a better way to be traditional? I realize this is way too far-fetched an idea for the traditional family-values folks. They also would be disturbed to find out that the universe is forever expanding. If they knew, they'd be devising ways to pour cement all over it. They believe in a God who likes things to stay the way they are, forever and ever, amen.

But I don't care. And neither should you. Because if the birth of the baby Jesus teaches you anything, it's that there are lots of ways to make a family—even to have God as your fertility specialist. For Neil this was the best way and really the only way.

People always say things happen for a reason, until they disagree with the reason it happened. I can't stand those kinds of people. I have never been big on the whole concept of things happening for a reason, but the reason here was crystal clear: it was a beautiful baby girl. Sophie.

If this weren't amazing enough, a few years later Neil and Machiko fell in love, and she found the whole arrangement completely acceptable—with a few adjustments, I would imagine. They got married and everybody is living happily ever after. (Sometimes you've just got to tip your hat to the life force.)

This is definitely not the way they do things on the Upper East Side.

What about the baby girl? She's growing up quite nicely with her two mothers and a father, thank you very much. Sophie is doing well in school. She doesn't need therapy or the myriad chemicals being administered to our children so they will sit still and learn. And she actually likes Jimi Hendrix and the Grateful Dead. Need I say more? From my vantage point, she has adjusted to what can only be described as an unusual family arrangement brilliantly. Maybe children are just a whole lot more fluid than adults realize. She certainly is more together than I am. My day goes up in flames when my coffeemaker doesn't work or when my editor says he doesn't like this sentence. *(EDITOR'S NOTE: Lewis, I never criticized this sentence. It's the paragraph I had problems with.)* It has never taken much to throw me off my game.

Life can be fucking strange and odd, and who knows, maybe you're better off if you learn that lesson when you're young. It might be the vaccination that helps immunize you from the bumpy twists and turns that life brings your way. It may be a little easier to deal with the weird stuff that life can hit you with if you've already had a chunk of it thrown your way.

Everyone involved in this story has been completely up-front about it. Which I find stunning, in a world where people hide their mistresses, sexual proclivities, and whatever else they can fit in their psychic closets.

The normal traditional way of creating a family seems to have freaked me out, so I can't even begin to imagine what I would have done in Neil's shoes. I certainly would have been unable to have leaped into the type of family that Neil has embraced. If I were in Neil's situation, I would have responded by looking for work on the Space Shuttle.

In the end, though, is this familial arrangement any more strange than the chemistry set that many have to pay for in order to reproduce? I am talking about the utter gymnastics required to get the borrowed sperm, the purchased eggs, the surrogate mothers, and all the pharmaceuticals in order to create a petri dish popover that will grow up to be the apple of someone's eye.

Not to me, at least not this family.

Once again, though, it just goes to show that most people want to procreate more than I do and will do anything to achieve it. I really don't get it.

And on Christmas Day I wonder: Have I missed the point of life on this earth?

"You're here," announces my Ugandan cabdriver.

I have found that Ugandans always have the answer. It's downright amazing.

CHRISTMAS DAY, 6:00 P.M.

Outeating the Christians; or,
Is a 10,000-Calorie Dinner Too Much?

❄

You'd think that after all I've said about this girl that I would arrive at Neil and Machiko's apartment with a wonderful gift for her. Nope. No birthday gift. No Christmas gift. I am in some form of gifting double jeopardy.

I promise you, I am really not a total prick. What I am is at a complete loss when it comes to knowing what a little girl might like for Christmas or her birthday. Talk about pressure. I don't have a clue what I want for my birthday, let alone my friend's daughter. They live in a completely different world from what I was brought up in, and what I now live in.

When I was a boy, girls played with dolls and Kenner Easy-Bake Ovens. You could really bake with them. You can still buy them, believe it or not. I don't know how the genius toy designers came up with this idea, as it is a lethal gift for kids. Shouldn't they be against the law? Not only because of the electricity that soars through it and the heating coil, but for dietary reasons. Toys shouldn't make kids fat. She's TEN YEARS OLD, what do you buy a ten-year-old girl? I haven't a fucking clue.

I know that I could ask her parents to buy her a gift. But I know they've already gotten her everything. Besides, she is a very sweet girl. She's not like Gus and Leo. She doesn't hold a grudge. That I know of.

When I get to Neil's, the room is abuzz with adults.

Machiko greets me: "Merry Christmas, Lewis, would you like a glass of Spanish Rioja?"

"Yes, I will have a glass of that delightful Rioja. Oh, this is excellent. Merry Christmas," I reply.

Another glass of wine, added to the glasses I had at Willie's, and it's apparent that the alcohol has begun to slowly take hold of me. Everything is taking on a slight glow.

I hug my very close friend Mark Linn-Baker, an exceptional actor. Like Neil, I met him at drama school. He has brought his daughter. Oh shit—another child I haven't bought a gift for.

"You are a stingy prick, Lewis," he says.

"I didn't know she'd be here," I say.

"Well, here she is."

"What was I supposed to get her?"

"A book would have been nice."

"A book? She's read *Harry Potter*."

"There are other books."

"*Nancy Drew?*"

"You're an idiot."

Yes, I am. I've known that for a long time. I never said I wasn't. Especially when it comes to females of all sizes, ages, and book preferences. Maybe I should have thought ahead and brought business cards that say: "Sorry, this is not my holiday." They'd ask me what was in those bags I brought. I'd explain that I have gifts for their parents. "Nothing for us?" they'd whine forlornly. And then I'd have to admit that even though they're great kids, I like their parents more. And no, I don't have to worry about them reading this. I have no intention of buying this book for them, either.

I'd tell them I gave a gift in their names to kids who have nothing and are starving to death. I'd tell them this, probably while my mouth was full of food.

Say, that isn't a bad idea, though. Next year.

Mark seems to be doing better than the last time I saw him. His wife is not with him. Their marriage, sadly, has been in the process of disintegrating. At times I have witnessed this at these Christmas dinners. I can't imagine it. I certainly had my own hell to deal with, but this is way different. They have shared the birth and the life of their child together. It's reason enough for me not to get married and have children. As if I needed another reason.

Unlike at Willie and Jenny's, the dinner here is more for friends than family. Each year, outside of Mark and me, there is a revolving guest list. All sorts of couples and singles have been in attendance over the years. They are designers, artists, restaurateurs, and businesspeople. Every few years another close friend of mine, Steve, the owner of the West Bank Cafe, and his wife, Janet, show up. They don't have children; instead they have a restaurant. (I think children may be easier. A husband and wife running a business together must be a tough road, but they do it with grace, style, and killer senses of humor. They need to have all three. Otherwise, they'd have tried to kill each other and I would have had to say something about them at their sentencings.)

The kids have their own table, which brings back memories. At holidays like Thanksgiving, my parents always had a table for adults and a table for kids. I always preferred sitting at the kids' table. I didn't need to listen to the adults prattle on about topics I had no interest in. The economy? Forget it. Politics? No thanks. Inflation? You've got to be kidding. It was a lot more fun playing with the muffins as if they were puppet heads than sitting at the big table, where you'd be reprimanded for playing with your food. Or blowing through the straw into your carbonated drink to make it bubble over the glass onto the tablecloth—now, that's entertainment. At the kids' table, you could be as goofy as you liked.

It's a good thing for me that the kids have their own

table, since at this point in my Christmas merrymaking the wine is taking a toll on my verbal-editing equipment. As you may have heard, I have a tendency to swear a teensy bit more than other people. The last thing that the tender young sensibilities need at Christmas dinner is to listen to me spout off about the load of bullshit that the douche bags are dumping on us because both political parties are so full of shit it's coming out their fucking eyes, or something equally thought-provoking and tasteful.

I should just shut up and concentrate on eating.

The meal is always wonderful. Prime rib. Can we please hear it for prime rib? I know the bovines and the vegans will be upset by this, but I can't help it. I love prime rib. I realize it's not as good for the cow as it is for me, but I'm sure she had a long and fun-filled life. I can tell by the way the meat cuts. Utter perfection.

I know this is wrong. Everything one does is wrong, when judged by someone who thinks it's wrong. And there's always someone who thinks whatever it is, no matter how innocuous, it's wrong. Even if most of the world thinks it's right. I mean, I get it. There are people who think eating meat is wrong. Taking the life of an animal is probably not the most moral thing to do. Even if you kill it in the nicest way imaginable, you are still killing it. If I am not screwing up one way, I am screwing up another. I was a vegetarian for a year. Not out of some moral choice, but because I wanted new stuff to taste. Except tofu. Fuck tofu. It's the lamest reason to chew. And in the end how do we know that vegetables aren't more intelligent and sensitive forms of life than those made of meat? We don't. Maybe they are an alien life form that is so advanced it's beyond our limited comprehension to recognize and we are seriously fucking up by throwing together a salad. And we are just not listening. I am sure there's someone somewhere who thinks it's ethically wrong to eat vegetables.

Eventually I gave up my vegan ways, not for any moral reason but because I missed meat. I missed the occasional burger. I found I had no interest in life if there was no barbecue.

Prime rib is a Christmas tradition in this household. There's a reason they call it prime. It's sublime when it's done right.

Neil always does it right. Steve loves the prime rib, too. He also loves the Subway meatball sandwich. It's amazing he has such a good restaurant, because his eclectic tastes go in some strange directions.

But even Steve knows a perfect prime rib when he tastes one, and this prime rib is perfect.

If that weren't enough, Neil also prepares pasta with a marinara sauce and hot and sweet sausage.

Not enough can be said about the joys of sausage. I love it at breakfast, though certainly not on a regular basis. But when it shows up at the evening meal, I weep with joy. And with an excellent marinara sauce and an unselfish pasta, it's a rhapsody. And with prime rib. Happy Birthday, Jesus, and yes I'll have another glass of red wine, pleeeeeeze.

No one should love food like I do. I approach food much the way a Christian approaches Christ. It sure makes me happy to know it's there.

The food is served and the wine flows. The dessert is excellent. I won't go into detail, because by now I am swollen—like a big blown-up tick. Conversations ebb and flow, cascading in crescendos over the table. We talk about what we are doing and what we're not. We laugh about how we are going to hell in a bucket but that it's all going to be okay because we'll be there together. Sure, the economy is fucked, but maybe in the long run that will be a good thing. We talk about the new drugs we're taking to control whatever conditions that age is bringing on. We talk about movies and books that we've seen and read or heard so much about that it's almost like we've already seen or read them.

We sing a rousing "Happy Birthday" to Sophie. I even sing it, and I hate singing it, but I owe the kid something, even if it's just my bad singing. It's nice to be with friends.

And, yes, I think one more glass of wine will do quite nicely. And why not? I have nothing to do tomorrow, except work on this book. I'm writing about Christmas, so fuck it.

. . .

After we've finished the meal, a woman arrives. She is introduced as a Single Woman.

"She's looking," one of the guests announces.

"For what?" I wonder. I mean, the dessert is there for the taking.

She starts to turn red.

"Well, she has three kids, and, technically, she's still married."

Technically?

"But she's getting a divorce."

Now everybody is looking at me. As if it's up to me to say or do something. As if everybody forgets that after the divorce, when she's technically single, she'll still have three kids, and so really she's part of a foursome. She's not single.

Shouldn't her friends let her relax for a bit, then revel in her newfound freedom, when she finds it? Oh, no. That's not the way these things work, Lewis. You can't be alone for a minute in this culture.

Lewis, you're available. Why aren't you interested in this woman you've known for exactly ten minutes?

Yes, I am single. Is there something wrong with that?

Well, yes, there is, because you don't have to be. So why are you? What is wrong with you?

In our culture, we don't really want single people around. I guess we make the whole social scheme messy.

If we are not with someone, then somehow we are creating chaos in the universe. We raise too many questions,
I guess. How come we haven't chosen to pair up? It
throws things out of balance. Noah brought pairs of
animals onto the ark; he didn't bring on any animal
without a mate. There was a reason for that. Maybe it's
hard enough to be judged for who you are, let alone to
be judged for the person you've chosen to be with. I
don't know. If I knew, I'd be with someone, goddamnit.

There is no real support in this country for people
who choose to be single. Of course one could argue that
they don't choose to be single, that by being by themselves, they somehow are getting what they deserve, but
for the purpose of my argument, let's not go there.

I perform at a lot of colleges, and although there
seems to be a new kind of dating, where males and females go out in packs, marriage still seems to be a high
priority for many of the young people I meet. If the
species and civilized behavior are to survive, it does
make sense that we are pushed onto the marriage-as-
monogamy track. As a result, though, most of us get married when we are under thirty, and the standard line
is that 50 percent of those marriages eventually end up
in the shitter. Is it crazy to maybe suggest that one
should learn to be alone before one learns to be in a
couple?

Is that really so nuts? For a country obsessed with the
freedom of the individual, it doesn't seem to apply to

being single. You can have all the freedom you want, just be sure to get married, for God's sake.

It took a long time for me to adjust to being alone. It may shock you to learn that I was never really comfortable with myself, and because of that I never got fully comfortable in a relationship.

Or maybe I'm just full of shit.

But if given a choice, most people, it seems, would rather be in a bad relationship than no relationship at all. As uncomfortable as it may be, there's a consistency to it that we seem to crave. It fills up the time as we ponder what the fuck we are doing in a shitty relationship. God knows, I have had my share of bad relationships, and God knows there were times I was the one who should have taken most of the blame for it being shitty. And most of the time I did.

The table has been cleared.

The other guests have left. All except me.

I have had a couple of espresso shots and am clearing my head with a little cognac.

It's Neil and Machiko and me and we do what we have done over the past few years. We discuss where we want to spend next Thanksgiving.

"How does Argentina sound?" asks Machiko.

"Don't cry for me . . ." I begin to sing.

I sound great. At least I think I do. I have risen from

my chair. Oh, no, I am singing and dancing. What is the matter with me, I don't even like the song.

Then I look at Neil and Machiko. They are stunned, and maybe a little horrified.

It's time to go home.

CHRISTMAS, 11:45 P.M.

Another Christmas Comes to an End, and Our Hero (Obviously Not Quick on the Uptake) Learns a Lesson

❄

After the day I've had, it's amazing I can walk. It's amazing I am able to climb into the cab. It's like exercise. I roll into it.

I am not so much drunk as bloated. If I were filled with helium rather than food and drink, I would make a perfect float for the Macy's Thanksgiving Day Parade. I have eaten more than any single man should at one sitting. I have eaten more than a small village should at one sitting. There is not enough Lipitor in the universe for me right now. I have been a piggy pig pig pig piggy piggy.

In my act I yell about idiot politicians and greedy businessmen, and yet here I am, just as idiotic and greedy. And on Christmas Day. Shame on me, for I am at this moment the fatty of the fattiest. I am not talking girth, I am talking filled to the brim. I am oozing blubbery lipids.

Years ago, when I was a young man just out of college, I would have mocked someone who had just spent the day as I had. (Well, not so much the amount eaten, but the foods themselves and the pricey wine.) I feel guilty about my self-indulgence and I begin to wonder what I should have done differently today.

Should I have given more to charity? Should I volunteer to be a volunteer at all of the places that need volunteers? Would that make up for all of this excess? I don't know.

How do you live a good life? I just can't bring myself to do what Jesus would do, which is to give up everything and follow his path. Why can't people do that? Why can't I?

And if I did, would it change anything, since Jesus himself didn't get much done while he was alive. Christmas isn't even my holiday and yet I get to celebrate a better Christmas than the hundreds of millions of impoverished Christians around the world. That's not right. Of course it isn't.

But right now, I am too bloated to do anything about it. (Jesus Christ, the cabdriver just hit a pothole and jostled me. I feel like I'm going to implode.)

. . .

And even though I'm feeling fat and remorseful, I know that what I did today was a great way to spend the day.

I just wish I could share it with everybody. But I don't like everybody.

If this guilt weren't enough, on the cab ride home, I go through all the failed relationships I have had in my life. How, Where, Why, When did I go wrong? What is it about commitment that leaves me uncommitted? Am I that much of a narcissist? Am I so self-absorbed that I cannot share my life with anyone? I don't know. Didn't these women who gave their love so freely to me deserve more than I gave back? Unquestionably. Do I really believe I am that much of a fucking prize? (Probably, but that's no excuse.) These were all women who were looking for a real marriage and a real family. And in every one of those relationships I had the best of intentions and I left them with what must have looked like the worst intentions.

I've managed to leave a trail of tears, and yet they were all lucky to be rid of me, I think.

"This is it," my Israeli cabdriver informs me. "And a Happy Chanukah."

As I ride up in the elevator, I realize that my software wasn't programmed for family life. It's barely programmed for this life, but whose is? Yet there are women

I know now I should have married, and I am haunted by regret. Their beautiful faces float across a river of memories. I mourn for the life I might have had and the children I haven't. There are no tears, just an overwhelming sigh as I open the door to my apartment. To the place where I live.

There are no children who are in desperate need of the attention I can't give them. "Daddy, Daddy, Daddy!!!" they would wail. And a wife crying out, "Where the fuck have you been? You said you'd be home by nine. The kids are making me crazy. You make me insane. I hope you had a goddamn good time."

There is nothing but the sweet sound of silence.

I am alone.

And to be honest, I am happy.

Once again, my friends have given to me more joy than they could ever imagine. I have shared their lives, and they are blessed for having them, and I am blessed for not. Every year they share with me the road I didn't take. Every year it reminds me that I just couldn't do it. As much as I know I have missed in my life, I fear I might have missed more.

It's why I write. If I am not going to be a father of a child, then I'd like to leave some messages behind to those who roll on through life behind me. It's like putting a message in a bottle and tossing it in the ocean that is time. If I am not going to have a child, I'd like to think of even this silly book as my legacy.

I realize I am married to my career. I am married to what I do. I am married to who I am. Maybe if I had spent more time alone and not out searching for my soul mate, things might be different today, but they are not. Maybe if I had reached some real success when I was younger, but I did not. It's the way it is.

And it's good. Very good. Oh, sure, I have regrets, but that's the nice thing about age. Regrets fade. And eventually, you die.

I realize I have given myself the best Christmas gift I could:

The ability to live my life on my own terms.

Of course, by morning that choice could bite me right in the ass, but for now, to be honest, I couldn't be happier.

And does that ever piss me off.

Merry Fucking Christmas.

AN ABNORMAL APPENDIX

The Chairman's USO Holiday Tour

In 2007 I got a phone call from a guy named David Steinberg, who is Robin Williams's manager. He said that Robin wanted to know if I would go on the USO Christmas tour with him and the Chairman of the Joint Chiefs of Staff, Admiral Mike Mullen. We would be performing at bases in Afghanistan, Iraq . . .

As soon as I heard Afghanistan and Iraq, I stopped listening.

"There's a war going on there, David. I'd hate to impede any progress we are making with my humor."

"Lewis, you're not that funny."

"Are you sure they want me? Did anyone tell the USO?"

"Yes."

"And they didn't flinch?"

"Not to my knowledge. They say they'd be thrilled to have you." That David is a smoothie. He can sling the bullshit with the best of them.

I didn't believe him. "Naaaaah."

"Yeeeeaaaaah. Do you want to go?"

"Of course I want to go."

"I promise you won't regret it. It will change your life."

It did.

My mother didn't want me to go.

"I will declare that I am on my deathbed if I have to," she said when I told her. "Lewis, what are you doing this for?"

"I am doing what I have to do for people who shouldn't be doing what they have to do," I said.

And I meant it. This is a request that you can't say no to. These people are our military. They do the job that so few of us want to do. They are literally putting themselves and their lives on the line so that I can argue with my mother about whether it's too dangerous for me to voluntarily go to entertain them for a few days. I owed them my time and whatever else the USO thought I could give to them. These are men and women fighting a war I don't believe in. But I believe in *them*. Though some idiots will continue to insist that you can't be against the war and for the troops, they are wrong. It's easy. It's easy because it's logical and moral.

It was one of the most extraordinary experiences of my life. When people ask me, what was it like, I compare it to a six-day LSD trip. Every time I turned around my mind was blown. I was living entirely in the moment, which is as exhilarating as it is exhausting. It's the kind of experience that words can't give enough meaning to.

The USO had set up a tour where we would spend one week entertaining troops in Qatar; Kuwait (Kuwait City, Camp Virginia, Ali Al Salem Air Base); Iraq (Al Taqaddum Air Base, Camp Fallujah, Tikrit, Baghdad, Balad); Afghanistan (Kabul, Bagram, Kandahar); Kyrgyzstan (Manas Air Base); Aviano, Italy; and Rota, Spain. In ONE WEEK.

I was allowed to bring one friend with me, to help out. I asked Steve Danielson, an excellent documentarian and friend. I never take pictures, or when I do they are awful, so he was going to keep a film and photo record of the trip. Also, he didn't have kids, and I just didn't want to bring someone along who had kids. As safe as it might be to be with the USO, they don't call it a "war zone" for the purposes of humor.

We left on December 16 from Andrews Air Force Base in Alexandria, Virginia, on Air Force Two. That's the plane that is second to Air Force One. *Air Force Fucking Two*, how good is that? It's the vice president's plane and is used by other hotshots who need it for an important reason, like transporting Admiral Mullen, or, as I like to refer to him privately, the Supreme Commander.

I take my seat on the plane and look over at the person sitting next to me. It's Lance Armstrong. Jesus, it's *Lance Fucking Armstrong*. I never thought our paths would cross. Why would they? I can't believe it myself. Oddly enough I have never qualified for the Tour de France, not even as a spectator. Facing us are Kid Rock and Robin. (The first two rows do actually face each other, so the bigwigs who are usually on board can talk strategy and stock prices.) *Jesus Christ.* Robin Williams, Kid Rock, Lance Armstrong, and Lewis Black. That lineup sounds like one of those "Which one doesn't belong?" questions that they give as an example because it *won't* be on the test because it's too easy. Those other three guys are iconic. Sitting next to them, I don't feel iconic at all. I feel laconic. And a little histrionic. But I keep that to myself.

I forgot the most important member on the tour, and certainly the sanest: the reigning Miss USA, Rachel Smith. She's stunning. How come I've got Lance sitting next to me and not her? He's no doubt thinking the same thing.

Lance Armstrong, by the way, is exactly what you think he is. He is physically perfect. PERFECT. He is a Spartan soldier come to life. Everything about him seems to be there for a reason. He looks fucking bionic, and it wouldn't have shocked me if during the flight he decided to replace an arm or leg with a new one. Sitting next to him, I realized that I was merely a rotting sack of flesh. If he's bionic, I'm gin and tonic.

He's got an ego, that's for sure, but he should. It's not obnoxious, he just exudes a sense that the universe seems to revolve around him. And why shouldn't it? He's *Lance Fucking Armstrong*. He rides his bike straight up mountains. He beat cancer. Beat it senseless. I wouldn't be surprised if he can see through walls. If I were he, my ego wouldn't fit in both Air Force One and Two. Shit, I wouldn't sit next to me.

Kid Rock is the personification of the rock-and-roller. He wears clothes that I would look like an idiot in. He has perfect hair. He has a swagger and a style that say, "Fuck you if you don't get me." So either you get him or you're fucked. Once I figured that out, I got him. It took a few minutes. Unlike me, Kid was gung ho for the wars in Afghanistan and Iraq. It was obvious I wasn't. We got into it for a little while. It didn't last long, as it dawned on both of us that we were on the same side. War or no war, I wasn't flying halfway around the world to show I didn't care, and Kid realized that. He'd been over there five times already. There are entertainers who are for the war, but they don't do shit. I admired him for putting his money where his mouth is.

Robin Williams is bubbling over, as he does from time to time. He's not always on, only when something touches his comic imagination, and then he's like a jack-rabbit examining every inch of the terrain he surveys. Later, when I asked something about Iraq, he gave me a clear, concise, and detailed history of the country. I mean, from its very beginnings. I've spent enough time with him to believe that his memory is not only photo-graphic, it's 3-D. He seems to know a lot about a lot. Or else he's an even better bullshitter than his manager, David.

It's a night flight, with a stop in Ireland to refuel (or maybe the pilots just want a pint of Guinness). When we wake up again we are in Qatar, which is a little bump of land along the eastern side of Saudi Arabia. That's right, we landed in the Persian Gulf.

As a Jew, I realized that I wasn't in Kansas anymore. (*Are* there any Jews in Kansas?)

I learned that there's a U.S. Army base there. No one is supposed to know we have a base there, of course, politics being politics. But of course everyone does. We're there to do a live show at a nonexistent base for the hundreds of American soldiers who aren't really posted on this nonexistent base. You figure that out.

I'd been in the air for fourteen hours, so I felt like I had been hanging upside down that long. It didn't matter how I felt, it was showtime. We had to hit the stage at ten a.m., local time. I have never been funny at ten a.m. NEVER! I can't even laugh until mid-afternoon. It's not easy to be funny at ten a.m. But if these men and women are willing to fight for me at any hour of the day or night, then I can at least pretend to be funny at ten a.m.

I give the show my best shot, so to speak. By noon I am already overwhelmed, and we've only just begun the tour.

The audience is a sea of khaki, from young to old, and by "old" I mean in their late forties, early fifties—men and women of every race, creed, and color. There are even a few elves and a couple of Santas.

After the show we eat lunch with the troops. We ask about their lives and where they're from and we talk about our hometowns. Even though my memory of the trip is a jumble—it's impossible to keep everything straight—I do remember that these kids humbled me deeply. They are so happy to have a little bit of the good ol' U.S.A. around them for a little while during Christmas.

After lunch, we immediately leave Qatar and head to Kuwait. Here's what I learned about Kuwait: women aren't allowed to drive a car in Saudi Arabia, so the Saudis bring their wives to Kuwait so that they can learn. Who knew? Who cares, you ask? Well, a few hundred thousand Saudi women who can drive, that's who.

Four hours later and we are back onstage. By now I am jet-lagged to the tits. I have been given no instructions on what to say, just a few hints about toning down the political humor, but I knew that already. You don't tell the troops that their commander in chief is a jackoff and a buffoon, particularly not in the middle of a war when you're just a few hundred miles from the enemy. I can do my bits on Republicans and Democrats, and I do. I do my bits on Christmas and Chanukah. Our show starts to take shape. The order is: Rachel, Lance, Lewis, Robin, and Kid. They love Rachel, Lance, Robin, and Kid. I'm not sure what they think of me. I know they like my foul mouth and my talent for inserting the word "fuck" in unlikely places.

We spend the night in a Radisson in Kuwait City. Who knew there was a Radisson in Kuwait? Even weirder, there is actually a Mexican restaurant nearby. You can get Mexican food in Kuwait. Small fucking world. Some of the folks go over for a meal. Me, I couldn't see eating Mexican food in Kuwait. I passed out just thinking about it.

We do two more shows the next day in Kuwait, and when we're done we fly into Iraq and do a third show.

It's about this time I come to the realization that I

could never have done vaudeville. Traveling from place to place, theater to theater, one after the other, it all becomes a blur of images, like one of those experimental films they show on a wall in an art museum. My memory, a poor thing at best, can only hold on to so many fragments of this USO tour. It feels like the afterburn of an LSD trip. But there are moments from this time that I do remember.

"Sweet Home Alabama" is one. I was never a big fan of this tune. I think it has a kind of a redneck tang to its lyrics. There's a great sense of longing in this song, but it's a longing for a time that has passed, and as far as I'm concerned it's just as well. But it's also a longing for a place, too, and that's what gives the song its grounding. Kid Rock plays it as his closer. When he sings it, it is transformative. He knows how to cut right through the bullshit that mires down the song with nonsense and hooey and goes straight to the gut and bone. Listening to Kid's rendition of it, the troops are no longer knee-deep in the shitstorm that is this war in Iraq. They are singing. Their faces are aglow with smiles. It's the rapture of rock-and-roll. Kid Rock has thrown a magic carpet out to them and whisked them home. Every time he plays that song, I cry. The roar that follows when he finishes sends a rush through my body. That roar is the sound of souls being freed from this earthly madness. It's the sound of a real Christmas.

.   .   .

There's a remarkable openness about our Supreme Commander, Admiral Mullen. Maybe it's on account of the way I stereotyped the military top brass from all those World War II movies I saw as a kid. I didn't expect Patton, but I certainly didn't expect such a nice guy with such a warm personality. And his wife, Deborah, is a doll. They could not have been more gracious or friendly to me. Me, who hates all authority. He spoke to me frankly whenever I had a question. He had a keen sense of not only the geopolitics of the world, but a sense of what would make our military stronger, and not in just a weaponry sense but also in a human sense.

During my time with him I saw him reading a book on Iraq and so I asked what it was and he said it was a book he wished he had read a year ago. He said that our time in Iraq has been a lot about catching up. That's as honest an answer as anyone who knows about America's role in the Middle East could have given, and I know he certainly didn't need to share it with me. But I appreciated it more than I can say.

I doubt the good admiral will like me calling him the Supreme Commander, but I do because I think it's funny. He has a tremendous affection for the men and women who serve under him. He spoke before each show that we did. He was as generous in describing us, the performers, as he was talking to the troops we were performing for. I wish they could shut down Congress for a month so he could give these idiots a workshop in leadership. Every single elected official on Capitol Hill could learn something from this thoughtful, committed gentleman.

Deborah Mullen's presence on the tour is just as important. She doesn't need to be slogging through a war zone with her husband. We know that, and so does she. But she did, and I'm sure the effect on our troops, seeing her take the time to be with them and talk to them, is powerful. It shows a true concern for those in uniform that is way above and beyond the call of duty. It's about humanity.

They have a really nice home on the grounds of the Naval Observatory in Washington, D.C. She could be at home, decorating the Christmas tree. But instead she's traveling with her husband through one of the most violent places on earth.

Performing in front of an audience when I knew she was there the first time was more than a little disconcerting. But I didn't hold back. I am sure these soldiers had heard the word "fuck" before. (It always amazed me that on Memorial Day a few years back, a number of local TV stations throughout the country refused to show *Saving Private Ryan* because when the boys hit the beach on D-Day, bombarded by artillery, some of them yelled "Fuck!" Who wouldn't? Did these idiots think they should be screaming "Sassafras!!"?) I am sure the soldiers use the word on a regular basis. I doubt, however, that Deborah ever has. By the time I finish my first set, I am positive she has heard more profanity in the last twenty minutes than she has in her entire life. I could sense her shock. But by the third show, she was laughing along with the troops. I wonder if she wanders around their home now, swearing for the fun of it. Doubtful, but it's a funny thought. I think she's happy that I made the troops happy. She knew that while my mouth may be in the gutter, my heart was in the right place.

On one of the flights on the tour, Deborah asked me to join her in the cockpit. (Now, there's a hell of a word. Who came up with that one?) We were on one of those huge jumbo carrier planes that the United States keeps building even though we have too many of them already. So I went up there to sit with her. The view was astonishing, not just the expanse of rock and sand and desolation that is Afghanistan, but the display of all those dials, knobs, and switches the pilots have to contend with. It's even more astonishing when, on the final approach, you overhear the two army pilots, who look to be about nine years old, arguing over which of the base's two airstrips is the right one. Deborah and I were scared just a bit shitless. You do NOT want to be there for these kinds of decisions. She didn't say anything, she just put her hand on my arm and dug her fingernails into me. It made me feel better, because the searing pain gave me something to distract me from what I wanted to do, which was to start screaming like a little girl.

To our growing anxiety, the pilots, as we got closer and closer and closer to the airfield, seemed completely unconcerned. Or maybe they were just fucking with us. As we were descending, the two of them finally agreed which airstrip to land on. Which was a good thing: you don't want to be remembered as the guy who shit his pants while sitting next to the wife of the Chairman of the Joint Chiefs of Staff.

We never made it to Baghdad that trip, and that pissed me off. You fly all the fuck way to Iraq, you want to see Baghdad. At this point it was all getting very blurry. We were doing our seventh show and it was only Wednesday. At the end of the show we were supposed to catch a flight to Baghdad. But when it was time to go, we were told that the weather was bad for flying. It had something to do with the wind and dust storms. As a result, we were going to have to miss Baghdad, where we were to stay at Saddam's palace—or one of them, at any rate. It was a bit of a blow to all of us. I wanted to see how a completely insane ruler lived. We all had personal reasons we wanted to get there. (The next year, we did make it to Baghdad, and we stayed at the palace Saddam had built in honor of his daughter's wedding. It was on a man-made lake, which Saddam had stocked with fish, because he liked to go fishing. There was a wall surrounding the palace that had been built to maintain privacy, and so that his subjects wouldn't know that Saddam had siphoned off the water that the farmers needed for their farmland so that he could maintain his lake. For his OCCASIONAL amusement and recreation, Saddam left the local farmers with arid land to till. In the buildup to the war, this is the kind of information that we might have been told. It certainly would have helped in manipulating public opinion. I guess just saying he was a meanie was enough. Oh yeah, and those weapons of mass destruction.

Since we couldn't get to Baghdad the first time, we had to stay at the base that night. Usually each of us had our own room. They were nothing fancy, but compared to the troops' quarters, we were living large. It turned out that because of a lack of housing, all of the guys were going to have to stay together.

Armed with this happy news, I walked into the very confined space. The whole experience brought back images of summer camp—WHICH I HATED! My mind was too fried to cope. The place felt claustrophobic, and I never feel claustrophobic.

Up to that point I had been able to take anything that had been thrown at me. But this was more than I could handle. In one small room there were six bunk beds. There was barely enough room to move around. Fucking stinking bunk beds.

That did it. The combination of a lack of sleep, the fatigue caused by the crazy performing schedule, and my own overloaded emotions made me snap. Severely. I had no choice, so I launched into a tirade at the poor girl who was in charge of us.

"You've got to be kidding me," I snarled. "This is it? This is where you want us to stay tonight? There are no other rooms on the base? I'll take a tent if you've got one. You can't put us all in here. There won't be enough oxygen in this confined space to get us through the night. For God's sake, we don't even have booze to make this seem like fun. Besides, I have a deep-seated fear that these guys will try and gang rape me, and who could blame them?"

The girl went into shock and scurried off.

Completely rattled, my brain was misfiring severely. Was this part of an experiment they were running on us? I wondered. Is this some kind of test to determine our psychological readiness for combat? (They could have just asked and I would have told them I have never been ready for combat.) If it was, then they needed to lock up the bazookas, because I was ready to explode.

By the time I calmed down, I looked around the room and noticed that there were only top bunks left.

FUCK!

I get up a lot at night. I don't sleep well, even in the best of conditions. And these definitely were not. Who knows what my shattered psyche would make me do in the middle of the night in a war zone? I could easily forget where I was and get out of bed and break a few limbs. I was a basket case.

Kid Rock was nice enough to exchange bunks with me. And I was nice enough not to tease him when he started reading a magazine article about Michael Jackson.

I was surprised when the girl I yelled at came back. By then we were all in our bunks. She announced that there was a couch in the TV room that I could sleep on. The ladies were all watching TV and I could join them.

Well, I am no little sissy-boy. I heard myself say: "I don't leave my men."

I actually said that. I don't think I have laughed harder at anything else that I have ever said. I was delirious. So was everyone else. Everyone was screaming with laughter.

When she closed the door on this group of men, we immediately reverted to being twelve-year-olds. Scattered farts shot across the room.

The fart is man's most basic form of communication. It's the way we say all is well, how are you?

. . .

Robin and I began to plumb the comic depths of our situation. The ensuing madness that occurred in this room is one of the funniest times of my life, and I can't remember any of it. Only the joy of men being so stupid, tired, and silly that we couldn't see straight, we could only laugh our tits off.

By early morning, we were off and headed to God knows where. Practically every place we went was God knows where. God and the people who call it home.

Humans adapt to anything. I can't. I couldn't even adapt to eight guys in a tiny room on bunk beds. I don't adapt well to long lines or automated operators or being put on hold and having to listen to bad music. I am a big baby. I admit it. Meanwhile, the men and women we were entertaining are struggling to adapt to a barren terrain, ungodly temperatures, and an enemy that wants to destroy you 24/7.

Oh, wait. Now I remember where we're headed.

Kabul. Which, it turns out, translates as "God Knows Where."

Every aircraft we get on is the loudest plane on earth, from the jumbo troop carriers to the small ones to the helicopters. Every one of them is fucking loud—louder than when I stood in front of speakers at rock concerts. But after three days, something strange happens: you get used to the noise. It doesn't matter anymore. I get on the plane and pass out. I don't know how our service people do it. Every time I see something new that they have to deal with I am more than amazed by their discipline. How do they hold it together? I'm just there to entertain and I am losing my mind about the accommodations.

And these people have families.

Yet they have a bond as a group that seems in some ways stronger than the bond of blood. It can't just be patriotism. It's got to be that every day they are living on the edge of death and they trust each other to keep them safe.

We roll into Kabul. It is a desolate place. It is a land of muted browns and grays and of cold that chills you to the bone. The Afghans walk by the side of the road. As we drive by in our car with an army escort, I stare at their grim faces. I am only a few feet from them but I might as well be a million miles away.

We hear later that there was a suspicious car that had to be dealt with on our route. We don't get much more information than that. There is security for us everywhere. The soldiers who watch over us are incredible, not just as protectors but as people. They go 24/7. They're always smiling. They seem to have a real love for what they do. I feel completely safe. Of course if they can't protect the Supreme Commander, then we are royally fucked.

We never see the enemy. If we do, we don't know it. At least I don't. And I'm paying attention.

While I'm in the Middle East there's an ABC News crew reporting on the war. Somebody asks to interview me about my experiences there. I agree. During the interview the reporter asks me to describe my feelings. I try but I can't. Instead I cry. I hardly ever cry.

It's snowing in Kabul and night has fallen. We are late for the show. We are always late. The schedule is tight. It would be a miracle if we ever kept to it. A few hundred troops have stood out in the cold and snow, awaiting our arrival. I don't know of any show I would wait for under these conditions, even when I was a kid. The outdoor stage is small and wooden. There is a sad-looking Christmas tree without enough ornaments on it.

It's still snowing, but once again it's showtime.

We are surrounded by a roar pouring out of hundreds of expectant faces.

The show was great, and Robin and Kid end with an improv blues number about being in the army and in Afghanistan. It destroys. To call the night magical doesn't do it justice.

It kept snowing. The audience was oblivious. Once again they were home. I was there, though. And I was freezing my nuts off.

We take photos with the troops after every show. Robin and Kid give as much offstage as they do when they are onstage. The troops surround Lance Armstrong. A few of the more intelligent guys gravitate toward Rachel. It's not like it was when the army was all-male. There are women everywhere. Rachel is beautiful, but in the world of today's army, she is not a complete novelty. I am sure during World War II, Korea, and Vietnam, the troops flocked to the actresses and models while Bob Hope practiced his golf swing and cracked jokes.

Even though we traveled thousands of miles, from one end of a war zone to the other, we don't see the dead. But every so often you saw a soldier who seemed lost or like he just couldn't take it anymore—whatever "it" was. Their stare is unsettling. Even when they're standing still, they seem to vibrate. I wonder if this is a war that is worth the cost of taking a man and making him hollow.

The most surreal moment of my entire time as a USO entertainer comes when we are in a chopper (I love writing "chopper"; it sounds so much better than "helicopter") flying us to another show. I've never trusted this mode of transportation to begin with, but to make it worse, the back of this one is open and a soldier sits at the opening with a mounted gun. I look out beyond him. There's nothing for miles. I don't have enough energy to imagine or fear that he might need to use that weapon to pick off an enemy. The gunner beckons Kid to join him. Kid gets up and walks toward the opening. We are flying over some areas where there are practice targets, and so Kid sits down and lets it rip. Then Lance does the same. The soldier beckons to me.

Are you fucking kidding me? Walk across a chopper toward a wide open space that is just beckoning for a body to fly out of it? Nooooooooooo, thank you. I didn't come to Iraq to watch Lance Armstrong, million-time Tour de France winner, or Kid Rock, guitar hero and rock star, fly out the back of a chopper. I also didn't want to make the nightly news back home and try to explain to a talking head why I didn't stop them or what I felt like as I watched them hurtle toward earth. Then we'd have to land and peel them off the desert.

Fortunately there was no drama. Despite my fears, it was just Lance Armstrong and Kid Rock firing off a few rounds of ammo into the desert below. The whole thing was nuts—too crazy for words.

I had to remind myself: We are at war. And those words are crazy enough.

.   .   .

A female soldier—I believe she was a sergeant—
explains to me that the problem is going to be when
these young troops go home. In Iraq, they have no booze
or sex. They have no outlets. They are going through
hell. They will arrive home ticking time bombs—the
men and the women.

During both tours, I meet a lot of National Guards-
men. As my friend the comedian Kathleen Madigan
says, this isn't the way it was presented to those guys at
the recruiting office. I doubt if a tour of duty in Iraq or
Afghanistan was played up in the brochures.

I spend some time talking to an army colonel. He's in
the Oregon National Guard. He was a gym teacher and
a coach in the school system there. He's already been
here for one tour of duty, then he returned home. He
started teaching again, and now the Guard has brought
him back. Maybe in World War II you ask schoolteach-
ers to go to war, but in this war? Really, is it all hands on
deck for this one? For Christ's sake, the guy is a *teacher*.
He teaches—shouldn't that exempt him? When they are
forcing us to take teachers out of the classrooms, haven't
the terrorists won?

I doubt the colonel would agree with me. He knows his men need him as much as his students do, if not more. I don't agree, but I've come to understand that this is the way a soldier thinks. He has to think that way. He has to when he is here.

I can't remember all of the hundreds of stories that the troops shared with me. I wish I could. Every one of them should be told.

There's one story I heard that has truly stayed with me. A woman soldier in her late forties and I began talking very early one morning, as she was policing the area. She had a friend, another female soldier, whose husband, another soldier, was back in the United States with their daughter. He had been called up and was going to have to ship out to Afghanistan. This will leave their daughter without a parent at home. Apparently having a child at home with at least one parent isn't vital to the welfare of the country. So the woman I was speaking to told her friend that she was set to go home—her tour was over—but that she would stay on so that her friend could go home in her place. Her friend still had five months left on her tour. She convinced the base commander to let them change places. Talk about "The Gift of the Magi." To put oneself in harm's way for a friend.

The woman's generosity took my breath away.

Now that, my friends, is a Christmas gift.

ACKNOWLEDGMENTS

Jake Morrissey, who fooled me into writing this book and whose advice was invaluable.

Hank Gallo, who has always helped me write a better book.

My parents, Sam and Jeannette, to whom I owe everything. And my brother Ron, who is always around even though he really isn't.

Willie, Jennie, Gus, Leo, Neil, Machiko, Sophie, Mark, Steve, and Janet for letting me write about them, and whose friendships I cherish.

Betsy Boyd, Kathleen Madigan, and Lenny Hughes for their input.

Shannon Kennedy, my assistant, who helps create space where there isn't any.

Frank Moreno, Jeff Costa, Ben Brewer, and John Bowman for keeping me sane.

Steve Fisher, my literary agent, for successfully scamming another book contract. Jim Gosnell and Jackie Miller-Knobbe, my agents, and Mark Lonow and Joanne Astrow, my managers, who had to deal with me writing this book.

Jim Yoshimura for his encouragement.

All my friends who have to put up with my nonsense.

Kosh, a visual artist of the highest rank, who gave me a great cover for my book.

Robin Williams, for inviting me to go on tour with him, and the USO for letting me.

Admiral Mike Mullen and Deborah and all of the other brass and security who were splendid hosts on both USO Christmas tours.

The West Bank Cafe—my resting place.

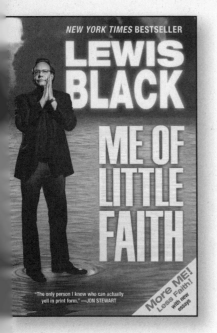

ALSO AVAILABLE FROM THE
NEW YORK TIMES
BESTSELLING AUTHOR

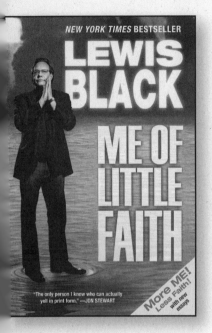

"The only person I know who can
actually yell in print form." —Jon Stewart

Available wherever books are sold or at
penguin.com

lewisblack.com

From Riverhead Books
A Penguin Group (USA) Company

T159.0611